ADVANCE PRAISE

"A brutally honest confession and road map that can help transform the culture of any system or individual willing to do the hard work of changing for the better."

—ESMAEIL PORSA, MD, MBA, MPH, CCHP-A,
PRESIDENT AND CEO OF HARRIS HEALTH SYSTEM

"As a diversity and inclusion practitioner, leveraging the insights from Love as a Business Strategy will propel companies into unchartered territories of success. Love is the most efficient pathway to achieving any form of success. If you and/or your company have the desire to evolve, you must read Love as a Business Strategy!"

—KANDACE COOKS, HEAD OF DIVERSITY
AND INCLUSION AT NURO

"Organizations founded on greed, power, control, and self-centered shareholder-maximizing strategies have not served us well. We need responsible and humanistic organizations that focus on human dignity and societal well-being. In this book, through the case transformation of Softway, the authors show us a compelling way to centralize humanity

in the workplace. *Love as a Business Strategy is real and much needed to transform the way we organize and lead our organizations. Through their examples and practical tips, the authors weave a story of 'love in the workplace.' This transformation is possible! It can be done. Love as a Business Strategy shows us how. A must-read for all managers, leaders, and C-Suite executives!"*

—DR. SHAISTA KHILJI, PROFESSOR OF HUMAN
AND ORGANIZATIONAL LEARNING AT THE
GEORGE WASHINGTON UNIVERSITY

"Love as a Business Strategy is the compelling story of one organization's gut-punch realization that success comes from embracing love as a core value."

—ROD BRACE, PHD, FOUNDING PARTNER
OF RELIA HEALTHCARE ADVISORS

"Love as a Business Strategy elevates what it means (and takes) to create a truly successful company. This is a raw, honest book filled with practical insights and inspiring stories."

—MARC EFFRON, PRESIDENT OF THE TALENT STRATEGY
GROUP AND *HARVARD BUSINESS REVIEW* AUTHOR

"Love is wanting nothing but the best for another person. Love is more than feelings and emotion. Love is action. Love is a verb. And Love as a Business Strategy provides a proven approach with simple actions any organization can apply to maximize their future growth by empowering their people to become the best version of themselves."

—JAMES ROBERT LAY, BESTSELLING AUTHOR
OF *BANKING ON DIGITAL GROWTH* AND CEO
OF THE DIGITAL GROWTH INSTITUTE

LOVE AS A BUSINESS STRATEGY

Love,
Moh A.

LOVE AS A BUSINESS STRATEGY

Resilience, Belonging & Success

Mohammad F. Anwar | Frank E. Danna
Jeffrey F. Ma | Christopher J. Pitre

LIONCREST
PUBLISHING

LOVE AS A BUSINESS STRATEGY
Resilience, Belonging & Success

ISBN   978-1-5445-2027-8 *Hardcover*
         978-1-5445-2026-1 *Paperback*
         978-1-5445-2025-4 *Ebook*
         978-1-5445-2028-5 *Audiobook*

To the past, present, and future employees and customers of Softway.

CONTENTS

FOREWORD

Dear Reader,

Writing this feels like a big task because there is so much I want you to know about the culture of love and the authors that have cultivated it at Softway. I think the fact that they entrusted me, a twenty-six-year-old project manager, to write this foreword says a lot about their character and the environment that they have created. This culture can be described in a lot of ways, but what it boils down to is one without fear.

There is no fear of making a mistake because mistakes are treated as learnings.

There is no fear of stepping on people's toes because we are all rooting for each other's growth.

There is no fear of speaking up because we know our ideas and concerns are always valued.

There is no fear of taking on something new because we know that we have support from anyone that we ask.

There is no fear of weaknesses because my weaknesses are supported by others' strengths.

There is no fear of leadership because the leaders share their mistakes with us with honesty and vulnerability.

There is no fear of the unknown because we trust that decisions are being made with our best interests at heart.

There is no fear of showing our true selves because we know that we will be welcomed with open arms.

For anyone who has lived in fear, you know that it is unpleasant at best and debilitating at its worst. When fear is present, there is no room for growth and maturity—you are simply trying to make it through the day. When you are able to let your guard down, that is where the magic happens. Those are the times when you are able to push beyond what you know you can do and accomplish things you never thought were possible.

I can't speak for everyone at Softway, individually, but I can say that I have heard testimony after testimony of this happening within our Softway family. Stories of extreme introverts taking over the microphone at all-company meetings, stories of people complacent in their roles and then pushed to take on a new challenge, stories of junior team members being given the opportunity to pitch to a client, and stories of a nervous project manager speaking on a podcast alongside some of the most senior leaders in the organization (thanks for believing in me, guys!).

It is our leaders who push us all to become the best versions of ourselves, and they do this by example—not by being perfect, but by sharing with us when they mess up. They are constantly striving to practice what they preach every single day, and they fail a lot, but they own it and attempt to better themselves because of it. I have learned so much from their vulnerability, simply because of proximity—lessons that I will take forward with me in my professional life as well as my personal life.

From Frank, I have learned the art of receiving feedback as well as the art of making a latte.

From Chris, I have learned how to make people feel heard as well as how to throw shade.

From Jeff, I have learned how to make complex problems seem simpler, as well as how a good game can bring people together.

From Mohammad, I have learned how to humbly apologize and ask for forgiveness as well as how to make really bad puns somehow funny.

I have not been a passive bystander in this culture of love. I have reaped the benefits because I have contributed to and sacrificed for this organization that I love. Sometimes that means forgoing sleep for a late-night or early-morning meeting to accommodate our team members in India. Sometimes that means doing things "outside of your job description" in order to get a project across the finish line. But a lot of times, it just looks like forgiving the leaders that I look up to because they too are human.

You cannot expect to experience a culture of love if you are not willing to be swayed and changed by that culture first. At the end of the day, what we have at Softway is special. It's not just a safe workplace. It's a home and a family. And like most families, we will get it wrong a lot, but that doesn't change the DNA that binds us all together.

With love,
Maggie McClurkin

OUR DARKEST DAY

The last few people filed into the large conference room, and the director shut the door behind them with an ominous *click*.

The crowd of employees looked around, confused. No one knew why they were there. After a pause that stretched out for what seemed like an eternity, an HR manager began handing out folders. One woman peeked into her folder and started reading. She looked as if she was going to cry.

A second director cleared his throat from the front of the room. "You're probably wondering why we called you here today," he said awkwardly. "Unfortunately, the company is going through a downturn. Effective immediately, everyone in this room is being let go."

Twenty voices erupted at once in shock and disbelief. The director allowed them a moment to react, and then he gestured for silence. Reluctantly, the crowd quieted down. "In a few minutes, security will arrive outside the room, and you'll be taken out in small groups to pack your things. Then, you'll be escorted out of the building."

A man in the front row scowled. Another asked, "Can I say goodbye to anyone?"

The director shook his head. "No. Anyone who is staying with the company is in a separate room. This is for everyone's protection."

"You can't just escort us out like criminals!" someone shouted from the middle of the crowd.

The director's face was set. "The folder in your hands has all the details you'll need. We appreciate your work. Thank you."

Angry voices flooded the room once more as the crowd erupted in unison. But as security arrived to escort the first group out, their protests gave way to resigned silence.

A woman came up to the director, hugging herself. "Why me?" she asked. "I'm good at what I do. I made it through the performance audit last month. Can you at least tell me why you picked me?"

The director looked at the woman, and then toward security, but they were occupied. Reluctantly, he turned back to her. "We needed to select a certain number of people. We did the best we could. There wasn't a reason you made the list. You just did."

"No *reason*? This is my livelihood! What do I tell my children?"

The director didn't feel good about brushing her off like that. But he had to say something. *Besides*, he told himself, *this is how they told me to do it. This is how you lay people off.*

He waved Security over when they returned, and they escorted the woman out with the next group.

The director let out a small sigh of relief. At least the hard part was over—though he knew he wasn't going to get a wink of sleep that night.

In fact, it had been a sleepless few weeks for many of the higher-ups at Softway, especially for Mohammad, the company's founder, President, and CEO. Since 2003, Softway, the company he had built from scratch, had been nothing but successful. It had brought in plenty of revenue and profitability, and had consistently seen strong year-on-year growth. From an evaluation standpoint, everything was trending positively.

Or so Mohammad had thought. About a month prior to the layoffs, Softway's executive leadership team called a meeting with Mohammad so they could deliver some shocking news: Softway was in a bad place. The industry was in a downturn, the company was losing contracts as a result, and they weren't bringing in enough new clients to make up the difference. If he wanted his company to survive, Mohammad would have to reduce his workforce by over a third—cutting ties with a full 100 of the company's 260 employees.

Mohammad slumped in his chair, stunned. "Okay," he said. "Tell me what I need to do."

As they walked him through the standard corporate layoff procedure, Mohammad's heart sank even further. It wasn't just the manner in which his employees were being let go; it was that he couldn't be directly involved in the process.

The executive leadership team was very strict on this—no one-on-one conversations, no apologies, no good-byes, and, above all, no actions or behaviors that might make him or Softway look sympathetic to his soon-to-be-former employees' situation.

"This doesn't feel right," Mohammad told his executives. "These are talented people who have done nothing wrong. It's bad enough they're losing their jobs, but do they have to be stripped of their dignity too?"

"This is the way it needs to be done," the executive team insisted.

Mohammad trusted these folks. He trusted their expertise, their backgrounds, and their previous successes. He made the decision to listen to their advice.

Mohammad assembled his management team—including Frank and Jeff—to help decide which employees would stay and which employees would go. The performance round would help identify some obvious cuts, but there weren't enough low performers to reach their quota. They would have to lay off some good performers too.

Then came the day of the layoffs. You already know how that part went, but what about the employees who weren't selected for termination? What was the experience like for them? The outcome was better (they got to keep their jobs), but their experience was just as bleak.

While the more unfortunate team members were learning of their fate on one side of the building, Mohammad, Frank, and

Jeff led the remaining team members to another break room on the other side of the building. That way, no one could see what was happening to their coworkers.

Once all of Softway's remaining employees were assembled, it was Mohammad's job to address the group to explain what had happened, and what the company's plan was moving forward. Facing the room, Mohammad swallowed hard and began to speak.

"You've probably noticed that some of your friends are not in this room with you today. That is because they are no longer with the company."

Mohammad went on to explain the tough situation Softway had found itself in. If the company hoped to remain in business, they would have to downsize. "But don't worry," Mohammad said, trying to sound upbeat, "if you're in this room, that means your job is safe."

"Yeah, for now," he heard a team member grumble from the back.

An hour or so of awkward conversation later, the surviving team members emerged from the break room and staggered back to their desks, stunned by how quickly the office had been cleared out. All traces of their former colleagues—their friends—were gone. It was as if they had vanished. Their desks were all cleaned out. Their access to their tech accounts had been shut down. Even their lunches were missing from the fridge.

It was only eleven o'clock in the morning. On a Monday.

And Softway had just endured the darkest day in its history.

BUSINESS AS USUAL SUCKS

If you picked up this book, this story probably sounds eerily familiar. In fact, we're willing to bet that you or your company have had at least one darkest day. You may have had several. One may be on the way.

If so, know this: you're not alone.

Stories like ours are far from unusual. In fact, all around the world, they're the norm. Just ask the executive leadership team who advised Mohammad on how to oversee his own layoffs. Every step was not only as cold and dispassionate as possible—but carefully planned out in intricate detail. They knew exactly how to handle this process because they'd been down the road before.

Let's be clear. While the story of Softway's darkest day may represent business as usual, that doesn't make it right.

Mohammad had gone along with the process his executive leadership team had outlined, but the experience changed him. Something had shifted in how he saw his company, in how he saw himself as a leader, and, most importantly, in how he viewed the team members at his company. From that point on, Mohammad began to question everything—including whether Softway even deserved to continue.

These weren't easy questions for him to ask. Since the day Mohammad founded his company, Softway had been a personal labor of love. He loved being in business for himself.

He loved growing it from nothing to an eight-figure company with offices in America and India. And he loved the CEO lifestyle and fancy Porsche it had afforded him. But he knew he wasn't perfect. After all, he was only twenty when he first founded the company. He had learned how to be an effective CEO on the fly, and as such he *might* have missed a lesson or two. This was why he recruited that executive leadership team of industry vets from IBM and Microsoft to show him how it was done and help guide his company to the next level.

This team was effective to an extent, but ultimately its members were concerned about only one thing: boosting the bottom line. And yet the more aggressively Softway pursued that bottom line—the more it pursued greed as a business strategy—the more it lost something far more valuable: its humanity.

Culture had never been Softway's strong suit. But in the months leading up to our darkest day, the environment was so lifeless you could hear a pin drop. Managers rarely interacted directly with team members. When they did, team members were treated like criminals. This didn't do our morale any favors. Across the board, Softway employees saw their jobs as purely transactional. They would show up, get their work done, and then count down the hours and minutes until they could pack up and go home.

If the environment we just described applies to your own company as well, be warned: these are the signs of a company living on borrowed time. Business as usual may have been good enough to keep our doors open and our bank accounts healthy for a while, but on our darkest day, our balance came due.

Fortunately, as bad as that period was, it wasn't the end of our company. In fact, since the layoffs in late 2015, Softway has learned not just how to survive, but how to thrive. And we did it by putting people at the center of everything we do.

We call this approach *love as a business strategy*. Through it, we have learned how to rediscover our humanity, put people at the center of work, and build a better business.

LOVE IS GOOD...FOR BUSINESS

In the following chapters, we're going to share the story of how we discovered and adopted love as a business strategy, what that pivot has created for us, and how you and your organization can do the same.

But first, let's address the elephant in the room: what is *love* as a business strategy? You'll get a complete description in Chapter 1, but in its simplest form, love as a business strategy means putting people at the center of work by creating a workplace that puts humanity first.

Here's why that matters: the average person spends more time with their coworkers than they do with their own families. For most people, then, work lies at the very center of their lives. That's a lot to ask of a person—and far too often, this sacrifice goes unacknowledged and unrewarded. Many organizations put little thought into the environment they create for their employees, which often results in an indifferent or downright toxic culture. Eventually, this culture starts seeping into other aspects of their employees' lives, affecting their health, their family life, their relationships, and ultimately their happiness.

It doesn't have to be this way. In fact, we believe that people and profit don't have to be mutually exclusive. The way we see it, there is not one number on a balance sheet that isn't connected to a human being. This means that if you want to produce better numbers over the long term, then you should support and empower the people *behind* those numbers.

We've seen what a difference this can make firsthand. When a group of motivated, talented people comes together to collaborate and create, they are capable of producing things far beyond the sum of their parts. Why? Because people who feel included, empowered, and supported are more willing to take risks, are more innovative, and are better at identifying hidden opportunities. In turn, they are able to produce better business outcomes.

This isn't just idle talk or well-intentioned theory. Through our people-first approach, both Softway and the companies we coach have seen quantifiable improvements across the board. Throughout the book, we'll lay out how the culture of love leads to stronger, higher-functioning teams; clearer, more attainable objectives; better business outcomes; and a healthier bottom line.

But while these results are real and important for the long-term success of any business, they're only part of the story. In our experience love as a business strategy is worth pursuing if for no other reason than it's the right thing to do. If the only impact a culture of love had was that it improved workers' lives both inside *and* outside of work, it would still be worth it.

LESSONS GROUNDED IN EXPERIENCE

This is not the first business book to discuss love, culture, or the importance of people. We acknowledge the input of so many others on our thinking, and we are indebted to their contributions. However, our journey has also helped us see things a little differently.

Since our darkest day in late 2015, Softway has become an entirely different company. We recognized that something needed to change, we committed to that change, and then we worked tirelessly to make that change a reality. Whatever we did before, we committed to doing the exact opposite—and that decision saved our company.

Along the way, a funny thing happened.

Inspired by our transformation, our clients began asking us our secret—and whether we could spark the same transformation with *their* organizations. Suddenly, love as a business strategy wasn't just something we practiced, but something we taught as well. These early pilot programs eventually led to experiences we call Seneca Leaders (an inclusive behaviors training program for leaders), which in turn led to a robust training and coaching program that we have brought to thousands of leaders and executives around the world.

Teaching love as a business strategy was never part of the plan, but it has become a natural outgrowth of the work we continue to do within our company.

Now, we're sharing those lessons with you.

This book is a collection of our lived experiences pursuing

love as a business strategy at Softway and teaching it to others. In the following chapters, we offer practical approaches, sensible solutions, and immediate applications for creating a culture of love within your business. These understandings, mindsets, and behaviors are realistic and achievable, if not immediate. Each chapter is designed for you to understand and apply what you have learned in a real and tangible way.

To begin your journey, we'll start with the basics. In Part 1, we take a deep dive into what we mean by love as a business strategy—what it means, what it means for your culture, and why individual behaviors lie at the center of it all. Then in Part 2, we introduce our Six Pillars of Love and discuss why they are essential in supporting a culture of love. Finally, in Part 3, we demonstrate how these concepts apply to different areas of your business—such as leadership, teams and individuals, diversity and inclusion, process and technology, business and people outcomes, and change management.

To bring these lessons to life, we will share stories of our own journey of discovery, both before we embraced love as a business strategy and after. Some of these stories detail our proudest moments, and some reveal our most embarrassing ones (try not to cringe too much when you read the story of Mohammad's infamous refrigerator email in Chapter 2).

We share these stories not to brag—and certainly not to embarrass Mohammad or other leaders—but to build empathy. We've experienced the cultural issues you're facing at your workplace, and we know what works—and what doesn't. By telling our story human to human, employee to employee, leader to leader, our goal is to help you connect with our message so that you can apply it to your own situation and behavior. By understanding the emotional component of our journey and what is at stake, you will develop a clearer understanding of what is needed to make lasting behavior change within your own organization.

Do we have the data to make a business case for love as a business strategy? Absolutely. But here's the thing: no one changes their behaviors because of data. They change when they understand the experience *behind* the data. Theoretical models of corporate structure and employee behaviors will never yield a living, breathing, adaptable culture of love. When you lead with numbers, you neglect the people behind them. But when you lead with people, you allow the numbers to take care of themselves.

Finally, this is a book for both leaders and aspiring leaders—for anyone who manages people or who expects that they might one day. While we often teach these lessons to leaders of mid-sized or large businesses across all industries, these lessons can apply just as easily to startups, small businesses, and industry giants. We can say without hesitation that Softway would have greatly benefited from a culture of love during its startup phase, and we have seen exceptionally large businesses, nonprofits, and healthcare companies find value from our teachings as well.

Organizations aren't the only ones that can benefit either. These stories, lessons, and strategies can also help at the individual level. As we've worked with other businesses, we've often found that both teams and individual contributors get great value out of changing the culture around them. We've especially found this to be true of middle managers, who, due to their unique position in an organization, have the most to lose by standing up for change. To those middle managers we say this: you may have the most to lose, but you also have the most to gain. After all, adding love to your work is a universal good, and the culture you create within your team can create a ripple effect throughout the rest of the organization.

Talking about love is easy. But delivering a culture of love in the workplace is hard work. As practitioners who have been at this for several years now, we can tell you that change doesn't happen overnight. In fact, you're probably going to see a few setbacks along the way. We certainly did.

But while change doesn't happen overnight, it *is* possible. And it begins by embracing your own ability to affect that change. Whether you're the CEO of your company or the newest team member, you have influence. If you can learn to wield that influence in the service of a culture of love, you will find value both for yourself and for your organization. In fact, you may even find, just as we did, that the impact you have is far greater than you could ever have imagined.

Part 1

WHY LOVE IS GOOD FOR BUSINESS

Do you enjoy working with jerks? Neither do we.

Even jerks that are really good at their jobs don't make work enjoyable (or even bearable). Sure, some may get work done, but they don't create an environment where innovation can thrive or where unique voices have a place to speak up and be heard. Do you think they are aware of how their behaviors affect others? Probably not. Are *you* aware of how your behaviors affect people around you?

The work of building resilient, high-performing companies starts at the individual level. This is why behaviors are the core of Softway's business philosophy. How we treat each other creates or destroys culture. In order to build what we call a *culture of love*, each and every member of an organization should be working toward improving their own behaviors—both for the betterment of themselves and for others.

Through introspection and self-awareness, meaningful behavior change is possible. Amplified by the Six Pillars of Love (which we'll cover in Part 2), we're able to achieve resilience and belonging, which in turn leads to our ultimate goal of high-performing teams and better business outcomes (lookin' at you, Part 3).

So here it is. Our secret sauce, on full display before you even turn to Chapter 1. But, as you're about to find out, there's so much more to the story. Mistakes and triumphs, highs and lows, our most stunning defeats and most epic realizations are nestled deep within these pages.

This is the philosophy we actively practice to cultivate a culture of love within the walls of Softway, and one that we share with clients and customers too. We have structured this book to mirror that same approach. Here in Part 1, we're going to start by tackling the foundational component of this philosophy: behaviors. But before we get there, we have to talk about the elephant in the room: What does love even mean?

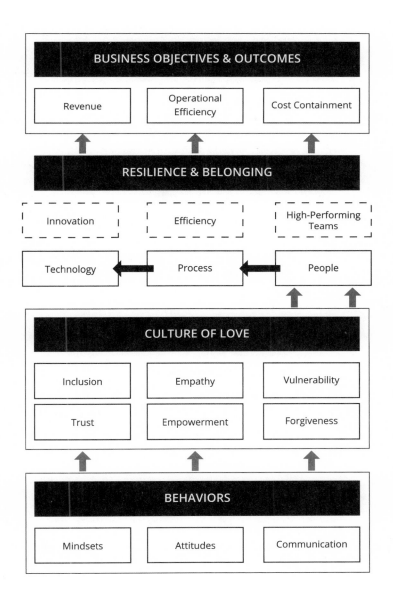

CHAPTER 1

WHAT IS LOVE? (BABY DON'T HURT ME)

In November 2015, Softway had its darkest day. Confronted with an unexpected downturn and desperate to keep his company afloat, Mohammad agreed to lay off over a third of Softway's workforce—around a hundred employees in all. This grim reality, coupled with the dehumanizing process of letting these team members go and the very real prospect that Mohammad might lose his company anyway, shook Mohammad to his core and led to a prolonged period of soul-searching.

It was in this introspective-yet-brooding mood that Mohammad found himself at a University of Houston football game (that's American football, for all you international readers) with his brother a few weeks after the massive layoffs at Softway. At the same time, the University of Houston—Mohammad's alma mater—was in the middle of a surprisingly successful season. Under the guidance of rookie head coach Tom Herman, the Cougars were undefeated and had just cracked the top twenty-five in rankings, according to an AP poll. On this particular Saturday afternoon, the University of Houston was set to square off against the University of Memphis Tigers. It was a big game, the biggest the Cougars had been part of in a long time.

A customer had offered Mohammad a pair of free tickets, and he had graciously accepted. Maybe this game would be just the distraction he needed to take his mind off his struggling company.

Or maybe not.

The first few quarters did not go well for the Cougars. After losing their starting quarterback early in the game (and with their second-string quarterback already on the injured list), the team was forced to trot out their third-string quarterback. Try as he might, the third-stringer couldn't keep his head in the game; he seemed just as surprised to be playing as the fans were seeing him play.

With less than thirteen minutes left in the fourth quarter, the University of Houston was down 14 to 34, putting their odds of winning at about 0.1 percent, according to the ESPN Game Tracker. Mohammad watched as the people around him began standing up and heading home, hoping to beat the traffic. He couldn't blame them. In fact, he had half a mind to do the same, but something inside him told him to stay to support his team. He knew a Cougar win was all but impossible at this point, but their whole season had been a miracle in its own right. Why not stick around a few more minutes to see if they had one more miracle left?

Mohammad's faith paid off. It was as if something clicked

among the Cougars down on the field, and they began playing like a team possessed. Over the next eleven-plus minutes, the University of Houston made play after play, pass after pass, run after run, until they pulled ahead by a point with less than 1:30 left in the game. Then, as the clock ticked down to zero, they were able to ward off a field goal attempt by the Memphis Tigers and hold on to win the game.

Mohammad, his brother, and the remaining crowd leaped to their feet, roaring in victory.

Greatest. Comeback. Ever.

When you witness a game like that, the experience tends to stick with you, coloring the way you look at everything else that's going on in your life. In Mohammad's case, he couldn't help but draw a parallel between the challenge the University of Houston had just overcome and the challenge he now faced at Softway. Here in November 2015, the company was both literally and figuratively in its fourth quarter. They were down by a lot, and the odds weren't good, but the game wasn't over.

However, for the first time in months, Mohammad felt a glimmer of hope that maybe, just maybe, Softway could pull off a miraculous win of its own. That night, he vowed to fight for the future of his company with everything he had.

On Monday, two days later, Mohammad was back at work, ready to start the week. Still feeling the high of the previous weekend's game, he logged onto Facebook so he could watch Coach Tom Herman talk about his team's miraculous victory at a press conference.

"You talk about how much these guys love each other," one reporter said. "We don't hear that a lot in the football world. Is that something you wanted to instill here? And is that something that helps win games—like this Saturday—and win championships?"

Herman agreed, saying that love was crucial to the Cougars' success. As he explained, Coach Herman had played on, played against, or watched teams that looked great on paper, but were only average on the field. "But to say that you are going to be elite or championship level in this sport without a genuine love and care for the guy next to you, I don't think it can happen."

Of course, the reporter was right: love isn't a word used very much in the game of football. So what exactly did he mean? "It's not, 'Yo Love you Dawg!' love," Herman explained. "It's a kiss you on your cheek, squeeze you real tight, and tell you, 'You have my heart in your hands' love....We're into real genuine love—and that's the only way I know how to do it. And it's the only way *we* know how to do it. And it's paid off so far."

Herman's comments stopped Mohammad dead in his tracks. He had never heard a coach—or anyone, for that matter—talk about "love" that way. But maybe he was onto something. Tom Herman, a first-time head coach, had guided his team to a 10–0 start to the season. And this wasn't a team of all-stars, either. By the most generous estimation, the Cougars had only three-star or fewer quality players on their roster. They had over-performed at every turn, and people were starting to notice.

Mohammad turned off the press conference and sat silently

at his desk. Was he like Coach Herman? Did he love *his* team? If he was honest, he had to admit that he did not. Mohammad could describe Softway's culture and his relationship to it in a lot of ways, but none of those ways included words like "love," "support," or "compassion."

But why not? Why couldn't Softway create a culture of love the way Coach Herman had for his Cougars? If love was the advantage the Cougars needed to become a winning team, why couldn't it be the business advantage that would drive Softway's own comeback story?

The more Mohammad thought about it, the more he saw love as a viable path forward. He wanted a team that didn't need to rely on star players to be excellent, a team that could overcome odds and take on any challenge, a team that radiated resilience, embraced challenges, and didn't believe in no-win scenarios.

And he was willing to do whatever it took to make it happen.

TIME TO FIGHT

On Monday, Mohammad heard Coach Herman use the words "culture of love" for the first time. On Friday, he was using that phrase himself in an all-hands company-wide meeting.

Everyone was gathered together for the call, with all the team members in America packed into the company's large conference room, and all the team members in India joining in over video. As everyone got settled, Mohammad took a deep breath, and began to lay out his vision.

First, he told them about the University of Houston football game. Then, he told them about Coach Herman's emphasis on love, and how he believed it was the difference-maker that created winning teams. Finally, he explained that from that day forward, Softway would be going all-in on creating its own culture of love.

"We need to love and support each other," Mohammad said. "That's the only way we will get through this."

At first, the assembled team members and leaders weren't quite sure what to make of Mohammad's speech, but they could tell he was dead serious—and deeply committed to taking his company in a new direction. No one was sure what a culture of love would look like, but they knew that pursuing it would change everything.

But while the path forward was uncertain, the change in the room was unmistakable. It was like a weight had been lifted off Softway's collective shoulders. Suddenly, it was okay to be optimistic again. It was okay to care. It was okay to feel inspired. It was okay to *try*, to batten down the hatches and fight not only for the company's survival, but for their team-mates' futures.

That Friday in November 2015 was a watershed moment in Softway's history. In the span of a week, Mohammad had found new inspiration in his role as a leader, recommitted himself to his company, and shared his heart with his team. He knew the road ahead wouldn't be easy—not by a long shot—but he was going to do whatever it took to get there.

Mohammad was going to fight, and he was going to win.

LOVE IS...

Since that November day in 2015, love has been at the center of everything Softway does, impacting not only our culture, but also our products and services, our relationships with clients, and even our position in the business world.

But, just as the artist Haddaway wondered in the popular nineties dance hit, we have to know: What is love? What exactly do we mean when we say we want to bring humanity back to the workplace?

First, let's get the obvious out of the way. When we talk about a culture of love, we aren't talking about office romance. In a business context, love doesn't have anything to do with romantic feelings at all. Love in the workplace isn't about hugs and kisses. In no way should a culture of love be misconstrued as an invitation to invite an HR dumpster fire to your organization.

Instead, when we talk about love in the business sense, we're talking about a deep-rooted and intrinsic care for other humans. Love in the workplace means working as a team with good communication. It means putting other people before yourself. It means looking to the person on your right and on your left and asking what is best for them as a whole person. Genuine, human care creates a ripple effect throughout everything people touch in an organization. It means focusing on humanity, not just profits.

...A RIPPLE EFFECT

Until Mohammad's fateful day at the University of Houston game, it wasn't love that drove our business. It was greed.

To be blunt, the massive round of layoffs we experienced in 2015 was merely the logical outcome of a poorly run company and an indifferent executive leadership team.

Driving this executive leadership team was Mohammad, whose own behavior may have been the worst problem of all. Most of the time, Mohammad would outright ignore the individual contributors on his team. When he did acknowledge them, it was either for purely transactional purposes or to yell at them for problems that weren't their fault.

If Mohammad's goal was to marginalize his employees and make them feel as if they didn't matter, then he was doing a fantastic job. It was no wonder, then, that the company's overall culture reflected Mohammad and the rest of the executive leadership team's behaviors. The camaraderie between employees was practically nonexistent. Smiles and banter were reserved for lunch breaks, when team members could get far away from the building and feel free to actually be themselves. No one had any sense of shared purpose in what they were doing. No one even knew the company was in trouble because no one had told them.

The more Mohammad embraced love as a business strategy, the more he understood that Softway's culture was merely a reflection of individual actions. As the president and CEO, his own behaviors had an outsized impact on the experiences and behaviors of others, and they were creating a toxic ripple effect throughout the workplace.

Humans come together to work, to collaborate, and to achieve beyond any single person's vision or ability. This is the real work that drives an organization's success, but none of this can happen in such a restrained environment.

Here lies the problem. Many of us don't stop to think about the kind of environment in which we find ourselves day in and day out. Sure, we may realize that the workplace can be a little lifeless, but what we don't realize is how dangerous that is. Silence is not a sign of work getting done. In fact, as we experienced firsthand, it's a sign of doom.

Fortunately, if a culture of greed is defined by individual behaviors, so is a culture of love. While the journey from love to a *culture of love* is complex and nuanced, it begins with individual efforts and behaviors:

Love means doing things out of care for others and with the intent of helping others, even if those things aren't easy.

Love means not sweeping problems under the rug.

Love means working toward inclusion rather than reinforcing hierarchy.

Love means embracing the hard conversations rather than avoiding them.

Love means building processes, tools, and policies that align people with profit.

Love means support, accountability, and trust, which leads to innovation, efficiency, and measurable business outcomes.

This isn't to say that a culture of love is all sunshine and roses.

In fact, as you'll see as you progress through the book, this is hard work. But the difference in your business between a culture of greed and a culture of love is the difference between a team of all-stars and an all-star team. Just as Coach Herman proved at the University of Houston, teams of individualistic all-stars rarely outperform teams of players who work together as a unit. Why? Because while all-stars often act in their own self-interest, all-star *teams* act out of love and a sense of mutual support.

WHAT IS YOUR WORKPLACE ENVIRONMENT LIKE?

As we'll explore throughout the rest of the book, pursuing love as a business strategy requires self-awareness and reflection about your own environment and behaviors. Here are a few basic questions to get you started:

- What does the environment in your own workplace look like?
- Is your workplace—whether physical or virtual—lively or silent?
- Do team members walk on eggshells around each other, especially around managers and leaders?
- Do team members spend long hours over-polishing presentations that decision-makers will barely pay attention to?

If your current work environment is heavy on politics but light on genuine interaction, if you find yourself spending considerable time thinking about how to speak with a coworker without upsetting them, then it's likely you don't currently work in a culture of love.

...SPEAKING TRUTH TO POWER

"You made me feel like I wasn't worth your time," Maggie said quietly.

Her supervisor, Chris, sighed. "I'm sorry I made you feel like that. You're right. You'd rescheduled the meeting twice for me, and..."

"...then you didn't show up at all. Without even sending me an email," Maggie said.

Chris stared at the floor. Maggie was right, and he knew it. More importantly, he knew better. By now, it was 2019. Gone were the days where this kind of behavior was considered acceptable. Chris knew he needed to make the situation right, but there was just one problem: he had a plane to catch. As much as it pained him to do, he had to leave Maggie waiting once again.

Maggie let out a sigh. That had not been easy. In fact, it had been terrifying. However, in her year as a project manager for the company, she had fully bought into Softway's culture of love. If she wanted to uphold that culture, she needed to know it was real. She needed to hold Chris accountable—and she needed him to understand how badly his actions were setting her back in her own work.

That night, Maggie told her roommate that Chris had stood her up for another meeting, and that, this time, she finally called him out on it.

Her roommate stared at her. "Wait, what?"

"What?" Maggie said, innocently.

"Chris, a vice president, who could hire you or fire you— that Chris? You really talked to a senior leader that way? Seriously?"

"Um, sure," Maggie said, a little uncomfortable. "What's wrong with that?"

According to Maggie's roommate, it was very wrong. "Sometimes, honesty isn't the best policy. If you want to keep your job, you're way better off staying silent."

Maggie was touched that her roommate was trying to take care of her—and in a normal organization her roommate would be right. Softway, however, wasn't a normal organization—at least, so Maggie had thought. *Had* she done the right thing?

The next day, a huge bouquet of colorful flowers arrived at her desk. The card was from Chris: "I'm sorry. You are absolutely worth my time."

Maggie smiled, brought the flowers home, and put the bouquet in her kitchen.

Most important of all, Chris followed up on his apology with action, making the next ten one-on-ones on time and without incident. (The eleventh he had to reschedule, but he emailed Maggie *days* in advance to move it.)

Maggie had done the right thing after all.

Many organizations would rather people be silent in front of leadership, but not Softway. We believe in love, and love means speaking truth to power, even if they're hard truths.

For Chris, Frank, Jeff, Mohammad, and the rest of our executive leadership team, what Maggie did was critical. If the Maggies of our organization lose their sense of safety and permission, then we as a company lose the ability to talk about real issues.

We'd rather spend our time addressing the problems directly, even if it means Chris has a stressful hour. It's faster and more productive and the people involved end up in a better place. The team member also gets the opportunity to share ideas that could change the course of our business for the better.

When we share this story with leaders at other businesses, they are often just as shocked as Maggie's roommate. To them, allowing their employees to speak freely endangers their authority. This couldn't be further from the truth.

Speaking truth to power isn't about challenging authority for the sake of it, and it's certainly not about giving leaders a piece of your mind. Love doesn't speak out of disrespect. Instead, it's about being receptive and empathetic. It's about approaching people as fellow humans, regardless of title or who is sitting in what chair. When everyone is on the same side, then everyone's contribution matters—and when everyone's contribution matters, then everyone will take care to communicate compassionately and effectively.

Speaking truth to power isn't just emotionally healthy. It's also more efficient. Consider your own experience for a moment. Has there ever been a time where you wanted to raise a flag within your company, but you weren't sure how to deliver the message? How much time and anguish went into planning out what you wanted to say?

If you're a leader, have you thought about what someone's silence is costing you?

In many organizations, team members are afraid to speak up for fear that leadership will see it as an accusation. So, rather than speak up directly, they spend an inordinate amount of energy figuring out how to get their job done silently, or to communicate indirectly and inoffensively in a way that still gets their point across. These environments cause team members to circumvent problems and circle around and around just to have a basic conversation. That's a lot of work, and a lot of effort and mental energy spent on essentially spinning your wheels. How exhausting!

When everyone is terrified of saying the wrong thing, then no one wins. Even worse, sometimes that fear can lead to illogical outcomes. Consider the story of the top-level executive who, after sitting through a presentation on a new branding design, said, "Huh. I thought that would be blue instead of red."

The executive was just thinking out loud, more curious than anything else. But because that organization's culture was rooted in fear, that one comment was akin to a four-alarm fire. Suddenly, entire teams within the company mobilized to change all the reds to blues—without anyone thinking to first start a dialogue with the executive on the matter. Did the executive *actually* want blue? Would changing everything to blue be more trouble than it was worth? What if red really was the right direction? How would they tell the executive he was wrong? Because no one thought to talk about it, no one would ever know.

In fear-based organizations, many conversations around strategy and behavior become events. You have to plan for them, use the right words, and have the right imagery. You have to make sure you're brand-compliant. You have to be so, so careful to say everything correctly and at the right time.

Why can't we just have a conversation without beating around the bush? Why can't we just be candid and not be offended?

Organizations that don't keep open communication channels, that don't encourage their employees to speak truth to power, are less effective and less efficient. Give your team members the space to feel safe enough to speak. Flush the issues out in the open so you can understand them, unite around them, take ownership of them, and then work together to solve them.

In a culture where you're encouraged to speak truth to power, success belongs to everyone, not just to leadership. The result is an engaged workforce that is invested in your organization's future. Everyone cares about cost containment. Everyone cares about sales. Everyone is committed to seeing the important numbers move, watching for trouble, and looking for opportunity. And when someone sees that something isn't right, or that something is objectively hurting those goals and values, they know without question that they are encouraged and empowered to speak up. If this sounds like a big lift right now, we get it. It *is* a big lift—but you don't have to do it alone. Solving the problems of a fear-based organization is what this book is all about.

...SHARING AND LEARNING FROM MISTAKES

At a campus Jeff once worked on many years ago, the company proudly displayed one of those "X days without an accident" signs. Jeff went past the sign twice a day, and twice a day he had a positive reaction when he saw any number larger than zero. It felt good to celebrate safe days on campus.

It wasn't until years later that Jeff realized how counterproductive those signs were. Rather than promoting safety, signs like that actually promote fear.

The core of this issue is what Harvard scholar Amy Edmondson has called *psychological safety*. Edmondson first coined the term during her work in the medical field, where she was researching the ways in which doctors and nurses worked together in teams. Initially, Edmondson set out to prove that doctors and nurses who felt safer with one another would have fewer incidents in their work. As she discovered, the opposite was true. When these doctors and nurses felt more comfortable with each other, they were more willing to share mistakes. Because everyone was learning from each other, they were less likely to repeat the mistakes that their teammates had made.[1]

Let's apply this lesson to Jeff's "X days without an accident" sign. Imagine you worked for this company. If you're the person who had an accident, how would you feel about resetting the counter? You'd probably be pretty embarrassed—perhaps enough to avoid reporting the incident!

This is what a culture of fear looks like. Accident counters like this may have good intentions, but they actually create the opposite results from what they're intended to produce. In a culture of fear, the accident *is* the failure. When people are afraid to even disclose that they had an accident, they fail to share any meaningful lessons they learned with the rest of their team, thereby dooming other teammates to make similar mistakes.

---

1   Charles Duhigg. "What Google Learned from Its Quest to Build the Perfect Team." *The New York Times Magazine*. February 25, 2016. https://www.nytimes.com/2016/02/28/magazine/what-google-learned-from-its-quest-to-build-the-perfect-team.html

A culture of love doesn't use counters and fear to encourage employee safety. Instead, it uses transparency and open communication. It encourages team members to talk about every safety incident openly—even the close calls—so that the focus is on learning rather than on blame.

As a company specializing in business transformation, we don't see many safety incidents at Softway. But like any company, we still make plenty of mistakes. However, because we operate from a perspective of love, we turn every mistake into learning opportunities. In fact, as Edmondson found in her own research, we've found that the teams that share their failures the most tend to produce the strongest results.

LOVE AIN'T EASY

When Mohammad called that all-hands meeting and took a stand for love, Softway's problems didn't magically disappear. Our culture certainly didn't change overnight. The transformation took time—and we're still working on it.

The important work always takes time. There are a lot of variables to account for. Like the rest of us, Mohammad had to learn what it meant to embody a culture of love, to establish it as the core strategy of his business, and to develop the mindsets and practices that would allow him to sustain the effort day in and day out.

More than that, it took time for Mohammad to generate the kind of buy-in that would lead to organizational transformation. It wasn't Mohammad's speech that was controversial. Nearly everyone in the company agreed that it helped clear the air and inspired the company to dig in and fight for its survival. However, there's a big difference between an inspirational speech and the hard, messy work of making the tenets of that speech the defining traits of your identity and culture.

Everyone loves a catalyzing moment. Everyone loves excitement and feeling inspired. However, once the big moment subsides, you're left with either empty words or hard actions.

Some folks at the company were certain it would be the former, that Mohammad was just riding a high from a great football game and that his enthusiasm would peter out in a month or so. They'd seen leadership wave at other flavor-of-the-month initiatives before, and they had little reason to think this time would be any different.

But when Mohammad started walking the talk, there was no longer any room for debate. For Mohammad, love meant business.

That's when the blowback began. Team members began constantly second-guessing Mohammad's actions and intentions. Many of them left—including the executives who had overseen the layoffs that led to our darkest day. They were unconvinced of the value of love as a business strategy and refused to step into a culture that actively embraced it.

Love as a business strategy is not built with words. It's built out of consistent daily action. It requires a focus on strong, inclusive relationships that are rooted in truth and mutual respect. It's a long process, and often it's a messy one. But it works.

As we stared down our own fourth quarter in 2015, worried

about going bankrupt, at times it felt like our odds were as bad as Mohammad's beloved University of Houston Cougars had been. At one point, we didn't even have enough cash in the bank to make payroll that week. However, because we committed to rebuilding our business around a culture of love, we clawed our way back. A year later, we were a profitable business again, and love had begun to take root in every aspect of our operation, from our strategic approach, to our culture and behavior, and to the very way we organized as a company.

A year after the layoffs, Mohammad wrote his company a letter. In it, Mohammad recounted the experience that had kicked off the company's journey of love and reflected on how far the company had come. Once again, he told the story of his experience at the University of Houston game, how he had left the game feeling fired up and ready to save his company, and how Coach Herman's emphasis on love had served as Mohammad's inspiration for Softway's own journey. The company had long since embraced his vision, but as Mohammad bared his soul to the company, the letter served as a crystallizing moment for the company, punctuated by these final lines:

> I hope you guys have enjoyed reading my story about how the Houston Cougars have inspired me! I look forward to reading your stories about who [inspired you] [...] and how you have adapted what inspires you to your lives.
>
> Take care and I love you all very much!!!

Just a year prior, Mohammad had looked deep into his soul and stared down an ugly truth: he didn't love his company and the people he worked with. Now, he was engaging his team members as if they were his best friends, sharing his greatest passions, encouraging others to do the same, and emphasizing his love and support for them.

For the rest of the Softway team reading this message, Mohammad's passion and sincerity were unmistakable. It was hard to believe that this was the same person who had once written the company a very different sort of letter—a letter that will forever live in Softway infamy...

CHAPTER 2

CULTURE EATS STRATEGY FOR BREAKFAST

It's lunchtime in the Softway office. You head over to the break room and open the fridge. After pushing a few things around, you find your food, head over to a nearby table, and start to eat.

A few minutes later, the CEO walks in. He seems distracted, as if the day already isn't quite going his way. He opens the fridge, mumbles something under his breath, slams the door shut, and walks out of the break room. *That's odd*, you think to yourself, *he didn't even take anything out. Must not have been hungry, I guess.*

You finish lunch and head back to your desk. After logging back on to your computer, you notice a message in your inbox from your CEO. Curious, you open it up—and instantly regret it:

Hello Team, It's really disgusting to see our fridge. There were items like Empty Bags, Last loaf of bread with mold, Empty Milk Cartons, Sauces, rotten bananas and these Boxes with food for DAYS AND DAYS all together... Really ?? Is this the hygiene you guys follow in your own homes? Disgusting! Here is the deal—We as a company are not required to provide you with a refrigerator. If you guys cannot take your own trash out the fridge on a regular basis.. I will not continue to tolerate this. You may do what ever you please with your own refrigerators. But you are not allowed to Softway's Refrigerators as your science experiment lab!!! I will give time till this noon for the folks who would like to reclaim their lunch boxes to take them or they will be thrown in the Trash!! This just demonstrates the lack of hygiene, discipline, and it shows How LAZY some of you guys can be to throw trash.. I mean EMPTY BAGS and EMPTY MILK CARTONS??? SERIOUSLY??? I also would like an acknowledgement reply to this email that you all understand that we need to keep our refrigerators clean by end of day today. The ones who do not respond to my email will have to help me clean the fridge tomorrow! Thank You!

Oof. That's not a good look. But hey, at least Mohammad said "thank you" at the end. (Yes, this is a real email Mohammad sent. We reproduce it here word for word.)

No doubt, you've received an email very similar to the one Mohammad sent out that day, whether from a fellow team member, a manager, or in our case, the CEO. The details may be different, but the result is the same: a toxic, dehumanizing company culture.

Mohammad got what he wanted out of this email. In the

hours after he sent it, there was widespread panic in the Softway break room as team members scrambled to clean up their mess—and then give the refrigerator a complete once-over to make sure everything was spick and span for their CEO. Of course, the refrigerator got dirty again a few weeks after.

While Mohammad may have gotten his way in the moment, it was a hollow victory—one that came at a tremendous cost. It wasn't just that team members were afraid to bring food to work now. It was that a large swath of the team had completely lost faith in their CEO and their company. We know this because they told us so (and the rest of the world) on Glassdoor. Just look at this glowing review:

> "The upper management is completely unprofessional. Expect to be ridiculed, yelled at, or cursed. You can also look forward to petty emails about the condition of the refrigerator with demands that you meet to clean it (which you may not even use)... If you see any good reviews, you can assume they're written by HR!"

There are plenty more reviews like this on Glassdoor and other sites. And while they're deeply embarrassing and hurt our ability to hire new talent, we also acknowledge that we earned those reviews, and we hold ourselves accountable to them. Mohammad's quest for a clean fridge cost Softway a lot of good workers—both at the time and in the future.

This was the state of Softway's culture in the months leading up to our layoffs in 2015. Softway was not a psychologically safe place to work, and it was our fault. Culture may be perpetuated by every team member in an organization, but it begins with leadership. Both in the now-infamous refrigerator incident and the many moments like it, it was clear that we as leaders had failed to produce and perpetuate a culture that we were proud of.

Without an intense, committed, and consistent focus on culture, love as a business strategy does not work. But in order to create a culture of love, first it's important to understand what exactly culture is and why it matters so much to a business's success.

CULTURE IS...

What exactly is culture? Admittedly, this can be a tricky question to answer. Here's our broad stab at it, and then we'll spend the rest of the chapter unpacking what that definition means and why it's so important.

Culture is about the *emotional* environment you create and the behaviors that build it—whether the environment is toxic or supportive. It's the passive-aggressive (okay, maybe just downright aggressive) email your CEO sends out about refrigerator etiquette. It's the way someone speaks to you in a meeting. It's the openness and ability of team members to give and receive feedback. It's the feeling among your coworkers propelling you to engage, to expect the best from yourself, and to support others in their work. Like the Force in Star Wars, culture is all around us, binding us together. We can't see it, but we can feel its presence in everything.

A poor culture plays politics all day. It rushes to get work done and go home. There's no camaraderie, no mutual support, no interest in anything other than performing your job at a bare-bones level. If your team members consistently dread going to work—if *you* dread going to work—then you have a bad culture.

A healthy, thriving culture, in contrast, is a *human* culture. People treat each other as human beings and are confident that others will treat them the same. They are empowered to make proactive decisions. They are entrusted to do the right thing. They are included and welcomed to disagree. They are free to bring their full selves to work, rather than a stripped-down version that leaves them complacent and unsatisfied.

Now that you have the thousand-foot view of what a healthy culture is and isn't, let's dive into some specifics.

...NOT PERKS AND BENEFITS

Here's a challenge for you: can you describe your company culture without mentioning your perks and benefits?

Companies love to showcase all their shiny bells and whistles to entice prospective employees to join their team. And certainly, it's great if your company has them. After all, who wouldn't want an on-campus ice cream shop, an amazing gym for a midday workout, or a ping-pong table in the break room?

However, as wonderful as all these things are, they are just features of your workplace—features that have very little to do with your company culture. Leaders focusing on perks and benefits alone don't create a workforce of engaged contributors. Instead, they create a hostage situation.

We know one person, we'll call her Anna, who stayed at

a job that she hated for over five years because she didn't think she'd be able to get those perks and benefits anywhere else. The irony, of course, is that Anna never got to enjoy the ping-pong table in the break room. She was too busy chasing deadlines and working long hours at her desk. In fact, whenever she heard someone else enjoying the ping-pong table, it made her blood boil. Still, as miserable as she was, for five years she didn't do a thing about it. She sat there, disengaged, and took a paycheck.

Finally, she left.

Companies that focus on perks and benefits generally have high turnover rates. As a result, they're stuck in an endless cycle of hiring new employees and conducting exit interviews. HR has to lie through their teeth every day just to recruit people into the company. (*Ask us how we know.*) What other alternative do they have? When you're working for a company with such a high turnover rate, eventually you run out of honest reasons to convince people to come in.

> Leaders focusing on perks and benefits alone don't create a workforce of engaged contributors. Instead, they create a hostage situation.

...GROWTH AND EMPOWERMENT

Famed business leader Peter Drucker once famously said that culture eats strategy for breakfast. What Drucker meant by this is that a well-conceived plan is meaningless if your team isn't united around that plan. They will struggle to execute and struggle to make proactive choices in service of organizational goals. Drucker put such an emphasis on culture because a healthy culture has an uncanny ability to motivate and unite people.

We agree that culture eats strategy for breakfast, but at Softway, we say that *behavior eats culture* for lunch. As we'll discuss in the next chapter, culture is the result of individual behaviors built up over time. In order to build a culture of love, each team member must have the wherewithal to understand their own behaviors and make proactive decisions in how they conduct themselves.

There are plenty of ways to measure the signs of a healthy culture. Broadly speaking, it all comes down to growth and empowerment. Healthy cultures encourage team members to bring their full selves to work, not the watered-down mask that the Annas of the world must grudgingly put on every day. Bringing your full self to work means you are:

Encouraged to communicate, be open, and share your perspective and ideas

Secure in the belief that no matter who you are or what your background, your contributions are valued and your voice matters

Able to be forgiven for mistakes and misbehavior

Able to give feedback, and receive feedback freely

In a healthy culture, there is no backstabbing and betrayal. Instead, you're—dare we say it?—*excited* to come to work, where you can apply your passion and skillsets in a way that is both engaging and fulfilling.

Is a healthy culture a workplace utopia? Of course not. Nobody wakes up excited to go to work every single day. No workplace has a workforce composed of flawless communicators. Practicing love and applying it to culture is messy. That's just part of being human.

However, the difference is that, in a healthy culture, when you wake up feeling dread about a particular aspect of your job that day, that feeling doesn't represent the entire experience of your work life. You may have messy interactions with a teammate, but you don't spend most of your time frustrated because you have the tools, resources, and space to address those messy interactions and grow from them. Finally, you may not feel passionate about every aspect of your job, but overall you believe that your work is engaging, your skills are put to good use, and the work you do matters.

Does your organization have a healthy culture? While culture may be hard to define, identifying a healthy culture is relatively straightforward. Ask yourself: if your organization was on the verge of closing its doors, would you dig in and fight for the company, or would you jump ship?

People will fight for places they believe in. Nobody but the owner fights for a business with a bad culture.

GAINING A FULL VIEW OF YOUR CULTURE

There's more than one reason to care about your company culture. With the rise of workplace review sites like Glassdoor and Kanarys, failing to live up to promises as a company can meaningfully impact your ability to recruit talent.

While Glassdoor has become the standard that companies are held against, other sites measure company culture in other useful ways. Kanarys, for instance, rates companies on diversity and inclusion. Many companies claim to care about diversity in public, but many fail to follow through on those promises in practice. For those in historically minority or underserved communities, this can be an invaluable tool in deciding where to work, offering a clear picture of a company's commitment to inclusion, and welcoming a diversity of voices to the table.

If you have big goals for HR, particularly around diversity in recruiting, be careful that your approach to diversity, inclusion, and company culture isn't just empty words. If you want to be known as a good place to work, you'll have to walk the talk. Otherwise, your reputation on Glassdoor, Kanarys, and other sites may hurt your recruiting experience and make HR's job much harder.

ANYONE CAN INFLUENCE CULTURE

Culture is embodied in people. It's the way you feel around your teammates. It's the way you engage. Culture happens in every interaction, and those interactions spread and set the tone for others. Day by day, action by action, we build each other up or tear each other down, and make space for others to do the same. Never is this more important than when we're talking about leaders.

Leaders have an outsized influence. Leaders set the tone. This is true in families, in business, and in politics. Every time a leader models the values and behaviors of a culture of love, their organization takes another step in a healthy direction.

Every time a leader misbehaves, the culture is damaged. There are no neutral interactions.

When Mohammad sent out his infamous refrigerator email, he wasn't just tearing his team down. He was pursuing a full-on scorched-earth policy. Anyone reading that email came away with a crystal-clear picture of what kinds of behaviors were acceptable at Softway in 2015: leaving a mess in the fridge was unacceptable, but publicly berating other team members was fair game. (Suffice it to say, we're glad our culture is different now.)

That said, leadership doesn't always happen at the top. If you're in middle management or an individual contributor on your team, you can still make a difference in the values and behaviors that you choose to model—with a tremendous impact on the culture of those around you.

Consider the example of Priyanka, a recruiter at Softway's Bengaluru office. For years, Priyanka had no interest in veering outside of her core competency. As she repeatedly told leadership, "If it doesn't say 'recruiting' on it, then I'm not touching it."

As Priyanka and other team members in HR shared their struggles and successes with each other, they realized that their insights didn't only impact the world of recruiting, but also payroll, communication, and leadership. This experience opened Priyanka's eyes. Today, she is a top performer in India's HR department, handling needs that extend well beyond recruiting.

Soon, HR began receiving messages from other Softway team

members like, "Man, I wish my team operated like yours. You have each other's backs. You really care for each other. You get it done." Soon, Priyanka and her team were offering support and coaching to other teams. Ultimately, this one culture change—driven by leadership, internalized by individual contributors, and evangelized within their teams—ended up having a dramatic impact on Softway's culture at large.

No one works with a thousand people every day. Most people interact with about three to five other team members on a daily basis, and perhaps ten to fifteen people over the course of a week. Every single person can have an outsized influence on those ten to fifteen people. Those people can influence their immediate contacts, and it can grow from there.

It doesn't matter if you have a company of a hundred or 200,000. Change still depends on individuals' actions. One person can change a team. One team can change a department. One department can change an organization. Progress isn't always linear; it's often uneven, and it does take time. But it can start with just one person.

ANYONE CAN ADAPT TO CULTURE

Frank gripped the passenger-side door in terror, barely suppressing a scream as his life flashed before his eyes.

Cars, bicycles, rickshaws, and pedestrians all competed for space on the narrow roadways. Screams, horns, and even the sounds of livestock filled the air. Everywhere he looked, Frank saw only chaos—and yet no one seemed bothered by it but him.

At the center of this chaos was Taj, Mohammad's brother,

who was laughing like a madman. Frank watched helplessly as Taj gunned the engine, hopped the car onto the sidewalk— on the *wrong side of the road*—and deftly wove between the many obstacles in his path.

Miraculously (at least to Frank), the pair arrived at the hotel. After taking a moment to collect his wits, Frank said, "What the heck was that? I thought I was going to die!"

Taj laughed. "That's how you drive in India."

He was right. In the context of his culture and surroundings, Taj's crazy driving (of which he is *very* proud) was entirely normal. In fact, it was essential. Had he driven more conservatively, he might have put Frank in even more danger.

These days, Frank understands this all too well. But after that fateful day in 2018, Frank vowed never to ride with Taj again.

Taj, the Managing Director of Softway's Bengaluru office in India, takes no offense. He may be a crazy driver, but he's also a leader. He understands how his driving must seem to outsiders. People from different cultures behave in different ways.

So when he first learned of Softway's pivot to a culture of love, Taj resisted. "That might work in America," he told Mohammad, "but there is no way it will work in India. That's not how Indians work."

Determined to make this culture shift work, Mohammad invited Taj to the United States for a visit. Upon his brother's arrival, Mohammad let Taj take the wheel and drive back to the office in Houston. It was as if a completely different man sat behind the wheel. *This* version of Taj obeyed the traffic laws, stuck to the speed limit, and flawlessly adjusted to driving on the right side of the road (rather than the left, as is the case in India). Mohammad couldn't help but point this behavior out to him. "Do you see how you're driving right now?" Taj nodded. "You were raised to drive very differently in India. And yet the minute you landed in Houston, your behaviors completely changed. Why do you think that is?"

Taj could see the point his brother was trying to make. If he could adapt to a different set of traffic laws in America than the ones he was accustomed to in India, then there was no reason to think that Softway's India division couldn't similarly adapt to a different culture. If an organization has its own defined set of values, behaviors, and culture, people will adapt to them.

This concept goes against many commonly held beliefs around regional culture. Just like Taj, leaders all around the globe often incorrectly assume that what works in their primary office won't work in their satellite offices in Europe, Japan, India, or elsewhere. So, they try to "adapt" to different regional cultures by superficially decorating their offices in an "authentic" manner. Then, when those locations inevitably run into cultural conflicts or contradictions, American leadership blames the problem on the actions or behaviors of people "typical" of that region.

Not only is this wrong, but it's also insensitive. No matter what larger culture their team members might belong to, no matter how many offices they have in different locations around the world, organizations can still build a company culture that is consistent both among team members and across locations. It has certainly been the case for us, as well as for the many other multinational organizations we have helped adopt love as a business strategy.

Still don't believe us? Consider your own behaviors for a moment. If you have a client-facing role, what do you do before visiting their office? If you're like us, you learn about their culture, norms, and safety standards ahead of time. If they require formal dress, you wear formal dress (even if the meeting is virtual). If they require that you leave your cell phone at the door, then you leave your cell phone at the door. From the moment you step on their campus to the moment you're back in your car, you automatically change your behavior in the way their culture demands.

Like Taj when he's in Houston, like us when we're client-facing (whether in-person or via video conference) if you can adjust your behaviors in different cultural contexts, then the rest of your team can too. No matter where your offices are located, no matter who the people are who work, every single member of your team is capable of behaving according to the values and behaviors mandated by a culture of love.

But for that to happen, those values and behaviors must be clearly articulated and enforced. Taj obeys the traffic laws when he's in America because the entire traffic system is designed to reinforce those laws. Further, he knows that if he circumvents those laws, his actions won't go unnoticed. When leadership sets specific cultural expectations clearly and consistently, people adjust accordingly.

So what exactly are the values and behaviors mandated by a

culture of love? We'll get to that in Part 2 when we discuss our Six Pillars of Love. But before we do, we need to understand the mindsets, behaviors, and attitudes that often stand in our way.

CHAPTER 3

BEHAVIOR EATS CULTURE FOR LUNCH

Just because we had pivoted to pursue love as a business strategy in late 2015, didn't mean we were suddenly a perfectly run business. With our leadership meetings, for instance, we still took what can best be described as a laissez-faire approach to scheduling. If Mohammad felt like having a meeting, then he'd send out an invite and expect attendance at the drop of a hat.

We also had a tendency to show up late. During one meeting in particular, nobody showed up on time. One member of the executive leadership team casually ambled in a minute late, then another showed up a minute later, click-clacking on her phone, and then another a minute after that. With each new arrival, Mohammad's face grew increasingly tense. He *hated* when people showed up late to meetings.

At ten minutes past the hour, Mohammad was finally ready to begin the meeting—until he noticed that Frank still wasn't there.

"What the hell is this?" Mohammad bellowed. "Frank is *never* on time for a single meeting. He has no sense of responsibility!"

The gathered team members shrugged. No one else knew where Frank was either.

Mohammad tried to bury his anger and start the meeting anyway, but he couldn't focus. Finally, after a frustrating few minutes, he'd had enough. He stalked out of the conference room and headed straight for Frank's office.

Mohammad burst into Frank's room to find him calmly sitting at his computer. Frank turned around to see a fuming Mohammad staring him down, but before he could say anything, Mohammad tore into him. "Why the hell aren't you at the meeting?" Then, he followed up with a flurry of words that, suffice it to say, we've elected not to put in print.

Frank blinked at him, surprised and disoriented. He sat up straight, tears filling his eyes. He mumbled an apology, then followed Mohammad to the conference room.

The meeting took place, but not much got done. With Mohammad shaking in anger and Frank sitting in a corner utterly bewildered, no one in the room found it especially easy to focus on any work. Eventually, the conversation wrapped, and everyone went back to their desks.

By now, Mohammad had calmed down a little and had begun to reflect on what he had just done. The more he thought about it, the more he worried that he had gone too far.

Sure enough, later that day, Mohammad's calendar pinged.

There on the screen was a calendar invite from Frank, requesting a one-on-one meeting. Moreover, he'd booked the meeting in the most isolated meeting room in the entire office, the room where people go when they're in trouble—or, even worse, when they're about to quit.

Oh crap, Mohammad thought as the reality of the situation set in, *is that what's happening here? Is Frank going to quit because of how I treated him?*

This wouldn't be the first time someone had quit over Mohammad's behavior, but he was trying to be better now. He was trying to inspire a culture of love, not perpetuate a culture of pettiness and anger. What had he done?

The next day came, and eventually, it was time for Mohammad and Frank to meet. This time, Mohammad was a few minutes late to the meeting, unable to settle his nerves and walk through the door. When he finally entered the room, he found Frank calmly sitting at the table. In front of him were his notebook and his closed laptop, and nothing else. Mohammad tried to make out what Frank had written in his notebook, but he didn't have a good angle.

Before Frank even said a word, Mohammad sat down and started talking—or rather, he started making excuses. He told Frank what a bad day he'd had before the meeting. He told Frank how mad it made him feel when no one showed up to meetings on time. He told Frank anything his guilty conscience could think of, though not once did he think to apologize.

"Mohammad, may I speak?" Frank said.

"Sure, sure, sure!" Mohammad sputtered out as he tried to calm himself and listen.

His hands shaking, Frank reached for his notebook and began to read. "I did not appreciate how I was treated yesterday. I did not appreciate the tone you used, the words you said, and the volume at which you said it. It made me feel disrespected and unsafe." Frank paused and took a deep breath. "I don't think that kind of behavior is what we're working so hard to create here."

Frank finished reading and put the notebook down, his hands still shaking. A long silence followed.

Finally, Mohammad sighed. "You know what, Frank? You're right. I'm sorry. I apologize. That wasn't okay, and it won't happen again."

Mohammad was sincere in his apology, but he worried it wouldn't be enough. Any minute now, he was sure Frank was about to resign.

"There's one more thing I want to share with you." Frank opened up his laptop and showed him his calendar for the previous day. As Mohammad's eyes scanned the list of invitees, one thing became painfully clear. Frank hadn't been late to the leadership meeting. He'd never been invited in the first place.

Mohammad began to think about the day from Frank's perspective. There Frank was, alone in his office and focused on deep work, when Mohammad burst in and began shouting like a madman. Then, once Frank was in the conference room with the rest of the executive leadership team, Mohammad had berated him again—this time in front of his peers.

"I had no idea what was going on," Frank said. "I only followed you into the meeting because I didn't want to lose my job."

"Frank, I'm so, so sorry," Mohammad said again as a fresh wave of shame washed over him.

So why hadn't Frank resigned? The thought had crossed his mind, but in the end, he chose to embrace the incident as a teaching opportunity instead. At this time, Softway was mere months into its pursuit of love as a business strategy. Frank had bought in fully to the new direction Mohammad wanted to take the company, and he wanted to give Mohammad a chance to actually do it.

If Softway was truly going to embrace a culture of love—whatever that meant—Frank had to be the person to step up and tell Mohammad what his behavior had actually felt like from the other side. Regardless of how Mohammad responded, it was Frank's responsibility to speak.

It didn't mean that anything about that meeting had been easy. In fact, it was far and away one of the most difficult professional conversations Frank had ever had. Confrontation is not in Frank's DNA, so confronting Mohammad in this way was *tough*. But, on the advice of one of Softway's VPs, Frank showed up prepared. He wrote down everything he wanted to say and how it had made him feel ahead of time and committed to approaching the conversation by being as cool and level-headed as he could possibly be.

It worked. Frank's bravery showed Mohammad the impact of his behaviors. From that day, we learned a crucial lesson. Culture may eat strategy for breakfast, as renowned business leader Peter Drucker famously said, but behaviors eat culture...for lunch.

Over the past few decades, companies have increasingly stressed the importance of culture in building a successful business. But while their hearts are in the right place, their focus is often unnecessarily broad, failing to account for the impact of individual behavior on culture as a whole.

Groups are made of individuals. As such, cultures are the result of individual behaviors. Each day, the behaviors of every single team member serve to either strengthen relationships or destroy them. And as their relationships go, so goes the organizational culture. The healthier the relationships, the healthier the culture. The more toxic those relationships, the more toxic the culture.

Here lies the key to successfully adopting love as a business strategy in your organization. If a culture of love is the goal, our individual behaviors are the path forward. In fact, we would argue they are the *only* path forward. A group cannot change if those within it are unwilling to change themselves.

So let's talk about our behavior—the good, the bad, and the ugly. This is a big conversation, so to help guide it we have broken behavior down into three categories: mindsets, attitudes, and communication. Mindsets are the foundations of our behaviors, attitudes are the way the world sees our mindsets, and communication is how we engage based on the mindset and attitude we're portraying at the time.

In the first part of this chapter, we'll explore each of these categories and how they impact our behaviors at work. Then, we'll wrap up the conversation by talking about misbehaviors—what it looks like when everything goes wrong—and set you on the path to aligning your behavior with a culture of love.

MAPPING MINDSETS

Every day you wake up with a perspective that orients how you handle the way you live. That perspective is called a mindset. Mindsets don't just affect your home life or your work life; they affect everything. All attitudes, communication, and actions ultimately have their roots in your mindset—how you perceive the world.

In her book *Mindset: The New Psychology of Success*, author Carol Dweck outlined two distinct ways of viewing the world: fixed mindset and growth mindset.[2] Whichever mindset you have, it affects your entire experience of the world—your actions, reactions, and interactions. For the purposes of this discussion, we're just going to touch on the key points. As you read through the following descriptions, keep in mind that no one is entirely one thing or the other. While each of us has a mindset we default to, anyone is capable of both fixed and growth mindset, and most of us bounce back and forth.

THE FIXED MINDSET

The core trait of a fixed mindset is that you are closed off to new opportunities. This could manifest itself in a number of ways:

---

2   Carol Dweck. *Mindset: The New Psychology of Success.* New York: Ballantine, 2007.

Fear: You constantly worry that you can't complete a task or do your job properly. As a result, you may be unwilling to try new things because you don't think you are capable.

Guilt and shame: A single failure overshadows previous successes. It is an eternal end state—no going back.

Persecution: It's you against the world, and you're in competition with everyone around you.

Scarcity: The success of others is a direct threat to you. The more they have and achieve, the less is available to you.

Judgment: You're constantly judging others, and you feel constantly judged. If someone makes a mistake, you see them as eternally incompetent (and you assume people would feel the same way about you if you make a mistake).

Inflexibility: Once you have made a judgment about a person or a situation, that's forever how you will see it.

As you might have guessed, the fixed mindset is incompatible with a culture of love. By its nature, it can lead only to behaviors that aren't inclusive, empathetic, or loving.

THE GROWTH MINDSET

The growth mindset is adaptable and resilient. The more problems you face, the more opportunities you have to learn— the exact opposite of the fixed mindset. Life becomes an adventure, not a pass/fail test. Common traits of a growth-focused mindset include:

Learning is key: It's not what you don't know. It's what you don't know *yet*. Every moment is an opportunity to grow, and so you're always willing to try new things.

Failure is temporary: Failure is not an end state, but a beginning. You're constantly looking for new ways to approach a problem, confident that one of them will lead to success. If nothing else, you will learn and grow from the experience. As Alain de Botton said, "Anyone who isn't embarrassed by who they were last year probably isn't learning enough."

Success is contagious: When you see others succeed, you're inspired, encouraged, and ready to cheer them on because you know their success is yours. Even better, when success is available to anyone, there's no pressure to compete.

Strengths take priority: You see others as intelligent and talented. Rather than defining others (or yourself) for their mistakes, you see your team members as resilient and capable of learning and supporting their teammates.

Vulnerability is strength: You are willing to be vulnerable in front of others because you assume others are there to help you rather than hinder you. By sharing your concerns, fears, and mistakes, you create a space for others to do the same—a crucial factor in creating high-performing teams.

It's probably obvious by now, but let's state it outright: a growth mindset is essential for creating a culture of love, boosting your chances of success, building resilience, and fostering an environment of learning. Without it, you may find that the attitudes you project don't align with the beliefs you hold.

Let's put these mindsets in the context of Mohammad and Frank's encounter. As you may have noticed, Mohammad's mindset going into that conversation was fixed. He saw time as a scarce resource that others were taking away, he felt persecuted when others showed up late to the meeting, and he judged everyone in the room (especially Frank) for it.

Now, here's the important part: when Frank confronted him, Mohammad didn't stay in a fixed mindset. The moment he realized he was in the wrong, he switched from fixed to growth. A fixed mindset, then, doesn't have to be, well, fixed. When Frank modeled an Influencer attitude (which we'll explain in a moment), Mohammad responded positively to that behavior, allowed himself to become vulnerable, and asked for Frank's forgiveness.

We should also note that Mohammad wasn't doing this consciously. While Softway may have already pivoted to a culture of love at this point in our history, the concepts of fixed and growth mindsets weren't yet in our vocabulary. We were still learning. However, because of our focus on building a culture of love, we knew that misbehaviors such as yelling, blaming, and shaming were antithetical to that mission.

ADDRESSING ATTITUDES

If your mindset represents the way you think, your attitude is the outward manifestation of that thinking. Think of it this way: if behaviors are a house, your mindset is your foundation and your attitudes are the walls, which others can see and interact with.

The way we see it, there are three essential attitudes: Flyer, Fighter, and Influencer. To understand how these attitudes might manifest, let's return to our opening story: Mohammad, Frank, and the missed meeting. As you will see, depending on what attitude Frank had operated from, it would have dramatically affected the outcome of that situation.

THE FLYER

As the name implies, the Flyer reacts to a fight-or-flight situation with flight. The Flyer may have the power or authority to be more proactive, but instead they choose to avoid the situation, complain, or adopt an attitude of victimhood.

Imagine Mohammad has just burst into Frank's office, snapping him out of the bliss of his deep work session. After Mohammad laces into him for a while, Frank responds by making excuses about why he wasn't at the meeting.

"I didn't have the chance to check my emails."

"Jeff asked me to work on something super-urgent."

"Chris distracted me with a Beyoncé meme he sent me earlier."

With each excuse and deflection, Frank the Flyer has created the conditions of his own victimhood. He does whatever he can to deflect blame from himself. Rather than confront the situation, he runs from it.

Of course, you know the real story—so you know that Frank really did have a valid reason for why he wasn't at the meeting. Despite this very good reason, Frank didn't deflect or otherwise run from the situation. In fact, he stood up, followed Mohammad into the conference room, and sat for the meeting (even though he had no idea what was going on!).

THE FIGHTER

Let's rewind the situation. Once again, Mohammad has just stormed into Frank's office and begun yelling at him. This time, Mohammad hasn't confronted Frank the Flyer—he's facing off against Frank the Fighter. The moment Mohammad calls him out for missing the meeting, he starts pushing back!

"What are you trying to say, Mohammad? That I'm lazy?"

Frank sneers. Of course, behind this tough-guy veneer, the truth is that, just like the flyer, Frank is afraid of looking bad. By leaning into the conflict, he's actually distracting Mohammad from the core issue—and therefore deflecting the criticism.

Aside from deflecting, sometimes the Fighter can outright distract. "Oh, like you're so great," Frank might say, "you can't even manage a consistent meeting schedule!" By pointing out Mohammad's flaws, Frank the Fighter hopes to look better by comparison.

THE INFLUENCER

Okay, enough dragging these fictional versions of Frank and Mohammad through the mud. If you couldn't tell, both the Flyer and the Fighter act out of fear—fear of being wrong, fear of being fired, fear of being publicly embarrassed, etc. The Flyer and the Fighter, then, are manifestations of a fixed mindset, focused on reacting rather than on learning. These types of mindsets create attitudes where individuals are unwilling to see the other side or participate in growth opportunities, which are once again antithetical to a culture of love. Once you become aware of Flyers' and Fighters' attitudes, you begin to see how common they are in a business setting—and how much they can impact organizational culture.

By contrast, our third attitude, the Influencer, arises from a growth mindset. The Influencer behaves the way you saw the real Frank behave in the story beginning this chapter. Confronted with a challenging situation, Frank sought out ways to support and teach others, as well as opportunities to better himself. In his case, Frank approached the situation with curiosity rather than with conflict, first seeking feedback from other team members on how to best approach the situation, and then inviting Mohammad to a calm, rational conversation (even if that conversation took place in the darkest corner of the office). In choosing this path, Frank the Influencer understood that even this problem had presented an opportunity for growth and learning, and he was much more interested in growth—his and Mohammad's—than in being right.

Of course, in the case of this particular conflict, Frank was in the right. But what if Frank had been in the wrong and actually missed the meeting? How might Frank the Influencer have behaved then? In short, he would have embraced the criticism rather than respond in fear. Instead of losing energy to drama, competition, and politics, he would have admitted he was wrong, asked for forgiveness, and committed to correcting his behavior.

This is why an Influencer attitude is so deeply aligned with a culture of love. An Influencer's calm and focus on learning extends around them like a gravitational pull. People want to be around that kind of energy. It becomes a physical manifestation of a growth mindset.

ARE YOU A FLYER, FIGHTER, OR INFLUENCER?

Just as we can alternate between growth and fixed mindsets, we can also shift among the attitudes of Flyer, Fighter, and Influencer, though we tend to default to one style. In some situations, we respond with fear. In others, we respond with openness and curiosity. Often, the reasons for our varied responses are unknown even to us. It could be that a particular situation triggers a strong flight response. Or, it could be that a certain person, for whatever reason, stirs the fighter sleeping within.

To a degree, these responses are out of our control. We may think we're responding as an Influencer, only to receive feedback to the contrary later on. As external manifestations of our mindset, attitudes aren't about how we perceive ourselves, but how others perceive us—and it can be difficult to know what that looks like without help.

During our Seneca Leaders workshops, we have designed an exercise with this goal in mind: to help attendees understand how others perceive their attitudes. First, each person is assigned an attitude. Then, when it's their turn, they act out an exaggerated version of that attitude in front of the group.

This exercise might sound straightforward, but many people struggle. Fighters struggle to be Flyers, Flyers struggle to be Influencers, Influencers struggle to be Fighters, and so on. The participant tries to portray one attitude, but the audience unanimously perceives another!

While this is only an exercise, it's an exercise meant to draw attention to an all-too-real dynamic in the workplace. Without feedback, many of us don't have a clear idea of how we behave at work. We may see ourselves as Influencers, while others see us as Fighters.

The next time you find yourself in an uncomfortable situation at work, take a moment afterward to assess your attitude. How did you see yourself in that moment? What did you do (or not do) that leads you to feel that way? Do you think others perceived your attitude the same way? Why or why not?

CONSIDERING COMMUNICATION

Still with us? Let's recap so far. Your mindset is something internal to you. No one else can see your thoughts or read your feelings. If you're afraid, no one can see that you're afraid. They can only see how your fear manifests through your attitude, which is the form and manner in which your mindset expresses itself to others. Now, let's add communication to the mix.

Both your mindsets and attitudes show themselves in how you communicate—which can often lead to mixed messages. For instance, you could have great intentions, and yet still communicate in a way that leaves a bad taste in your coworkers' mouths. Alternatively, you could have not-so-great intentions but communicate in a way that makes others feel good. In a culture of love, neither of these outcomes is ideal—each represents a form of communication breakdown.

To understand what's going on in these moments, first let's start with the two core types of communication:

Intrapersonal: This is internalized communication or communication within yourself. For instance, after Mohammad barged in on Frank and started yelling at him, Frank could have told himself the story that Mohammad was out to get him. He could even have told himself this story over and over again, until Mohammad's mere presence triggered a Fighter response, causing Frank to cut Mohammad off or dismiss his ideas.

Interpersonal: This is communication between two or more people, whether verbally, in writing, or through body language. Often, it's the combination of verbal and nonverbal cues that people perceive. For instance, Mohammad could have said to Frank, "I think it's really wonderful that you weren't at the meeting on time today." However, if he was grinding his teeth while he said it and pacing around the room, Frank would rightfully interpret that statement as being sarcastic or otherwise insincere.

To communicate successfully, it's important that you're mindful of how you communicate both intrapersonally and interpersonally. In other words, it's important that you're (1) mindful of the stories you tell yourself, and (2) aligned in your mindset, attitudes, and communication so that you can communicate authentically with your team.

Here's the thing with inauthentic communication: it's hard to keep up. It's easy to think that you can just put on a mask and hide what you're feeling, but masks crack. The facade is all but impossible to keep up. Eventually, whether through verbal or nonverbal cues, people will see through the mask to what you really feel. Maybe your voice will crack. Maybe you'll catch yourself scowling when you meant to be smiling. Even if these cues only last a moment, those moments speak volumes.

Fortunately, authentic and genuine communication is just as plain to see—and in the long run, it requires far less energy. Why put in all that effort to maintain a cracking mask when you could just admit that you're upset and ask for a moment to calm down? As we'll see in a few chapters, that kind of vulnerability will benefit you in ways the mask never could. Sure, taking a step back feels like the opposite of progress, but in reality, it will get you further than pretending ever could.

UNFORGIVENESS: THE ROOT OF ALL MISBEHAVIOR

Now that you understand how mindset, attitudes, and communication come together, let's bring this conversation back to the main topic of this chapter: behavior. When you behave supportively, you contribute to a culture of love. When you behave destructively, you strip away that culture.

We all misbehave at one time or another. However, if we are to grow from these moments, if we hope to turn down the misbehaviors and turn up the positive behaviors, then we must first understand them—and where they come from.

Misbehavior comes in many flavors. While the following list is far from exhaustive, these are the misbehaviors you're likely to encounter (or exhibit) in the workplace:

Verbal attacks: These were the old Mohammad's specialty, whether it was yelling in a meeting, cutting others off, or sending "nasty-grams" about refrigerator etiquette via email.

Emotional abuse: These are often mistaken for verbal attacks at first, but in effect they cut much deeper. These piercing statements are meant to make the recipient feel dumb, slow, or incompetent. They may be phrased as a joke, but they land like a ton of bricks. Emotional abuse is usually deployed to stop an argument dead in its tracks, often under the guise of "showing you how I feel" or "putting you in your place."

Apathy: In the workplace, apathy often manifests through variations of the silent treatment. You ignore a teammate by pulling out your phone. Or, maybe you continually find ways to avoid a topic or a particular conflict. From a leadership perspective, it can mean neglecting to give a team member important feedback through one-on-ones or coaching sessions. You're not invested enough in their success to help them.

Disassociation: This is the weaponized version of apathy. Instead of simply behaving indifferently, a disassociated person actively ignores others, refuses to give them work, or refuses to ask them for help—even if doing so is to the detriment of the project and the company.

Mind games: We like to joke that the modern practitioner of mind games was the designer of complex torture devices in medieval times. At their core, mind games are overcomplicated and manipulative, designed to get something you want while avoiding any responsibility for the outcome. One common mind game is a concept known as *gaslighting*, whereby a person deliberately denies, misrepresents, or omits critical information in order to confuse another person into believing they're in the wrong. To a practitioner, mind games often feel like justice. But to those on the receiving end, they are anything but.

Financial repercussions: In the workplace, financial repercussions could mean denying someone a promotion or pay increase. Or, it could be more subtle, such as reducing a team or department budget as a way of getting back at someone.

All the misbehaviors are common in workplaces around the world. However, only one of them—financial repercussions—is actively taught in MBA programs. Chris was taught in business school that if a leader doesn't want to confront a person on their team, the solution is to put that person on an impossible assignment. That would force the "undesirable" person to either quit on their own or fail—in which case the leader would have grounds to fire them. Suffice it to say, such behavior has no place in a culture of love.

While all these misbehaviors manifest in different ways, they all stem from the same root problem—what we call *unforgiveness*.

To illustrate what we mean, let's turn once again to the story of the Missed Meeting. When Frank first confronted Mohammad about his misbehavior, the first thing Mohammad did was blame other people—in this case, leadership's tendency for being late to meetings. This is often the telltale sign of unforgiveness. It's never your fault, but someone else's:

"I was stressed."

"Jeff made a mistake, so I had to do what I had to do."

"Chris tried to humiliate me."

"Yeah, I yelled at Frank, but it was to teach him a lesson."

We've all said things like this. And we all know that, deep down, they're just excuses. Nevertheless, we find ourselves going to elaborate lengths to justify our misbehaviors—all because we couldn't find it in our hearts to forgive someone (or often, to forgive ourselves).

Here's the thing about unforgiveness: it's most likely to rear its head in the relationships we care most about. Why? Because those relationships have history—and no history is all sunshine and roses. In this case, the old axiom is true: familiarity really does breed contempt. This is why we'll go out of our way to apologize for bumping into a stranger on the street but yell at a family member for doing the same thing. It's not that we love the stranger more. It's that—even if we don't mean to—we have a lot of unresolved anger toward the people we love.

The same phenomenon happens in the workplace. Slowly over time, we get into the habit of disregarding our close coworkers' feelings. Then, after the first perceived slight, we begin to take their goodwill for granted and start allowing ourselves to misbehave. We may write this off as innocent, but it's not. The more familiar we are with another person, the better able we are to hurt them. With each misbehavior, with each act of unforgiveness, we chip away at our culture until there's nothing left.

WHAT'S YOUR FAVORITE WAY TO MISBEHAVE?

During our Seneca Leaders workshops, we ask participants to choose which misbehaviors they default to. Many pick apathy or disassociation. When things get hairy, they simply disconnect. Participants are far less likely to admit to verbal attacks, emotional abuse, or mind games—even though, if you look at any workplace, these particular misbehaviors are just as common as any other.

As you consider what your own go-to misbehavior is, you're likely to find two answers: the misbehavior you want to do, and the misbehavior you actually do. We tend to deny the former and only focus on the latter, but with a little digging, you can get at the truth.

Our participants who choose apathy often choose to identify with this misbehavior because of their tendency to ignore coworkers they don't like. But here's the thing: ignoring someone is also a sign of playing mind games. The question is how do you tell the difference? In this case, ask yourself a follow-up question: Does it matter to you if the person notices? If no, then your go-to misbehavior really is apathy. If yes, if you then change tactics afterward, then, whether you realize it or not, you like to play mind games.

It's not easy facing down our own petty sides. (We know from experience. Just ask Mohammad how thrilled he is to see so many of his own misbehaviors in print!) However, once you understand your own misbehaviors, you're in a position to contextualize and come to terms with them.

In the early stages of understanding, you will be tempted to associate misbehavior with an external trigger. Someone else was incompetent. Someone else scared you or pushed you out of control. However, dig deeper into your own reactions. You'll nearly always find unforgiveness at the root. You will have resentment from a present situation or a past one that's being hit. You're holding someone hostage in your head.

INTRODUCING INTROSPECTION

Here, at the end of Part 1, you should have a good understanding of what love looks like in a business sense, how love is ultimately expressed through culture, and how culture is the sum total of individual behaviors. Further, you should understand the mindsets, attitudes, and communication patterns that inform our behavior. You should also have a good grasp of what misbehaviors look like, and what triggers them. Now that you understand all the components that contribute to a culture of love, you can begin to rethink your own behaviors with clarity and intention—and in so doing help bring love to your own workplace.

In Part 2, you'll begin this process of transformation as we take you through our Six Pillars of Love. But before we get started, there's one last piece of the behavior puzzle we want to address: introspection.

In business, we're more accustomed to reflection than true introspection. We might reflect on a meeting we had, our department goals for the quarter, or the year's fiscal results. Often, these moments of reflection are framed in terms of performance: What did we do well? What could we have done better?

Reflection is useful, but it's only a surface-level assessment. After Mohammad yelled at Frank over the alleged missed meeting, he reflected on his behavior and concluded he had misbehaved. However, it wasn't until after Frank confronted him that he thought to look within himself and understand the reasons he had misbehaved. *Why* did he get angry? *Why* did he think it was okay to treat Frank the way he had? Questions like these are the work not of reflection, but of introspection.

Introspection means thoughtfully assessing where you are, what needs to change, and why. Such a process is naturally time-consuming—which is why it's not as widely practiced in the workplace as it should be. That said, introspection is essential to building a culture of love. If you really want to change your behavior, you must understand why you behave the way you do, and more importantly, what you can do differently.

Effective introspection requires a few key components:

Gather feedback: You can't rely on someone like Frank to book a one-on-one with you every time you misbehave. You can, however, connect with others to learn from your experiences, work on uncovering your true motivations, and understand the root causes of your behaviors. From there, you can work on corrective actions that will yield meaningful results.

Consistency: Introspection isn't easy to maintain. It requires a prolonged focus on your own motivations and actions. If you start by considering why you got angry, but then you veer off into thoughts about how no one shows up to your meetings on time, you've lost the thread. You are blaming rather than introspecting. Maintain the focus on yourself and don't get distracted by other factors.

Accountability: It's all too easy to say you're a good person, and to think that as long as you have good intent, nothing else matters. The reality is that intent doesn't matter. People can't see intent. Actions will drive how other people perceive you. Don't allow intent to become a "get out of jail free" card. Focus on what happened, why it happened, and what you can do about it either now or next time a similar situation arises.

Patience: Many people put off the work of introspection because they feel as if the process never ends. (Hint: it doesn't—although you can reach useful stopping places.) However, if there's one single thing holding people back from lasting behavior change, it's that they don't do the work. While the work of introspection may never end, it does come much easier with practice.

If there's one thing you take from this chapter, it's the importance of introspection. Nothing else we've discussed in this chapter will happen as quickly or as well without first cultivating this ability. There isn't a whole lot you can control in this world. You can't control the weather. You can't control whether your company succeeds or fails. You can't control the behaviors of those around you. But you *can* control yourself and your behaviors.

Is any of this easy? Absolutely not. Often, the work of introspection can feel as if you're staring into a black hole. The act of introspection might bring up painful memories from your past that you'd just as soon prefer to leave buried.

If you're not ready to go that deep, then you don't have to. Every little insight, however small, is still useful—not just in your work life, but in your whole life. After all, triggers don't disappear when you leave home or when you go home. You can't separate your humanity from the person you are at work—that's the whole point of love as a business strategy.

So do the work. Don't let yourself off the hook. Ask yourself the hard questions. Spend the time to consider your mindsets, your attitudes, and your communication.

The only way to create a culture of love is the hard way. But if you can commit to the process—if you can commit to *your-*

self—then you will have unlocked all the tools you need to make it a reality.

Part 2

UNDERSTANDING THE CULTURE OF LOVE

By now, you have a good foundational understanding of what a culture of love is and how individual behaviors can either create or destroy it. Here in Part 2, we're going to start building on top of those concepts with what we call the Six Pillars of Love.

As you move through these chapters, here are two things to keep in mind:

First, while we've laid these pillars out in a specific order here, in practice they are interrelated and interdependent.

Inclusion, for instance, depends on trust, empathy, and vulnerability in order to succeed.

In that way, these pillars are much like the cylinders of an engine—you need all six firing in harmony in order to create momentum and move forward. If even one cylinder is firing out of sync, performance suffers—and it may even fail.

Second, these pillars all represent words and concepts you've heard before. In fact, you may even be tired of hearing them. We understand, but we also ask you to keep an open mind. The stories we use to explain the pillars of inclusion, empathy, vulnerability, trust, empowerment, and forgiveness are told through a practitioner's lens, driven by our lived experiences, mistakes, and triumphs. As you read, try not to skip the explanations or jump ahead, but instead ask yourself: "How can I apply this pillar to myself? What would this look like in practice around me?" You might even discover some pillars that your organization is missing entirely.

CHAPTER 4

INCLUSION

Imagine stepping into a work environment feeling that you don't have a voice. Imagine feeling belittled and small, disengaged from your job and pushed aside. Now, imagine literally traveling to the other side of the world—enduring nearly twenty-four hours of flights and layovers—just to feel that way.

Until 2016, this is exactly how our Indian teammates felt when they traveled to Houston. We know because they have told us. Unfortunately, it took us far too long to ask for that feedback and listen to what they had to say.

In fact, this issue wasn't even on our radar until the first time Chris traveled to India. From almost the moment he arrived, Chris was struck by how well his Indian teammates went out of their way to accommodate him. They picked him up from the airport. They took him shopping for groceries and essentials. They took him out to dinner. They even cleared their weekends just so they could show Chris the sights and sounds of Bengaluru. When he first set foot in the Bengaluru office, one of his fellow teammates even offered Chris his lunch—and came close to forcing it into his hands as he walked toward a meeting!

Chris loved feeling welcomed and included, and he appreciated the efforts his teammates had made. But the more he had time to reflect on the experience, the more he realized that this amazing treatment only extended in one direction.

When Indian team members came to the United States, they weren't treated nearly as well. In terms of hospitality, all our Houston team was able to muster was a lift from the airport—and even that didn't happen every time. There were no grocery runs, no dinners, no weekend fun, and definitely no team members eager to offer up their lunch.

Before Chris's visit to India, very few people at Softway had considered the experience of team members visiting from our other office. What we had been doing—leaving people alone, isolated, and largely ignored—was antithetical to a culture of love. We were thinking only of ourselves. Once Chris understood the problem, he knew it needed to stop.

Changing company habits was going to take some work. In fact, as soon as Chris set out to reimagine our visiting employee experience, he realized he didn't even know where to start. So, he reached out to a few Indian team members to find out what their experiences had been like in Houston and how Softway could have made them better.

Many of the visitors reported having difficulty sleeping their first night in town. For this group, that first time in the company apartment was like the night before the first day of school. They had waited their whole lives to visit America, and now that they were here, they had trouble calming themselves down and getting a good night's sleep. But, as Chris suspected, that excitement usually gave way to a different feeling: isolation. Softway's Indian team members had to figure out everything on their own—where to eat, where to get basic supplies, and even where to get a haircut. In the office, visiting team members from India were mostly ignored, often made to spend meals and breaks by themselves in one corner of the break room. They felt fundamentally alone the entire trip, and often voiceless.

To correct this, Chris implemented several new policies. First, Softway began creating welcome baskets for all visiting team members—complete with a towel and a mug to sip their favorite chai. Also included in the baskets were a variety of American snacks that are popular among our Indian team (honey toasted pecans are always a big hit). Finally, the baskets are capped off with a series of personalized welcome notes handwritten by US employees. When visiting team members enter their room in the company apartment, these welcome baskets are there waiting for them, allowing us to make early connections with them and give them a few conversation starters for their first in-person meetings the next day.

Chris's efforts didn't stop there. He wanted our Indian team members to feel as good as they made him feel. So, he made sure that a Softway team member would always be at the airport to offer a ride, take them out to dinner (or pick it up if they were too tired), and help them secure supplies. Finally, it is now company policy that Houston team members make time to show their counterparts around—whether that's taking them out to a nice Cajun dinner, inviting them to a Beyoncé and Jay-Z concert, or taking them to a local monument.

All of this might sound like a lot of work (it is), but it's the least we can do to make each and every team member at Softway feel welcome, valued, and, most importantly, included. That's what the first of our Six Pillars of Love is all about—making sure that everyone in your organization (and everyone you invite to visit) has what they need to speak, contribute, and bring their full selves to work. There's a lot of nuance to matters of inclusion, as well as its antecedent, marginalization. And approached haphazardly, efforts to address issues of inclusion and marginalization can be ineffective at best, and actively damaging at worst.

WHY INCLUSION MATTERS

In companies that don't explicitly emphasize inclusion, many team members feel as if aspects of who they are might not be welcome or appreciated—as if they aren't allowed to be their full selves at work. As a result, they hold back important parts of themselves that could potentially add value to the organization.

A culture rooted in inclusion, however, enables everyone to contribute at a high level. A fully included team is a more productive team, and a more productive team produces far better business outcomes. However, creating space for that full inclusion can be a challenge. Organizations must look for opportunities to include, and to establish a place where team members include, even when it's more convenient and less costly not to.

Effectively ignoring our visiting Indian team members was an easy choice because it required zero effort. Behaviors such as picking them up from the airport, creating welcome baskets, and showing them the local culture, on the other hand, are *packed* with effort. But it's precisely *because* the actions of inclusion require effort that makes them so valuable: it is a way of telling our team members that their needs matter to us, and that we have taken them into account. If that means some of us have to take a little extra time out of our days, so be it. The alternative—making someone feel uncomfortable, uncared for, or otherwise marginalized—is not an option.

Inclusion and belonging are basic human needs. When we meet that need at work, we create a better world in microcosm. For that reason alone, inclusion is worth it. However, an inclusive organization is also a more effective one. Executed consistently and effectively, inclusion leads to innovation and creativity, empathy, retention, the benefits of diversity, and resilience. It allows more voices at the table and gives those voices permission and comfort to speak. It creates loyalty and a sense of belonging, which makes team members fight harder for the organization and for each other. In short, inclusion unlocks strong teams and individuals working to their full potential and firing on all cylinders.

THE DIFFERENCE BETWEEN
DIVERSITY AND INCLUSION

Terms like "diversity" and "inclusion" have become big buzzwords in the corporate lexicon. But while many organizations emphasize diversity and inclusion (commonly referred to as D&I), far fewer are able to point to tangible results from their efforts.

Why is this? One reason is intention. D&I training is often undertaken for the wrong reasons—specifically, to avoid lawsuits. Unfortunately, when D&I is only code for CYA (a cheeky industry abbreviation for "cover your ass"), then the training often creates more bias than it solves.

Another reason is that the terms are often used interchangeably. To be clear, diversity is not the same as inclusion—nor is it simply a box you can check off in the hiring process. While diverse hiring practices are important, all the diverse hires in the world will not benefit your organization if you make no effort to make them feel as if they belong.

At Softway, for instance, we address this by representing people of different backgrounds and different levels of seniority in key meetings. We recognize and acknowledge our need to hear from divergent thinkers or those with unique perspectives. Otherwise, why would we have put so much emphasis on hiring them in the first place?

Lastly, another reason D&I efforts fall flat is that they often fail to address the core issues. Even an organization with good intentions might not realize that their hiring, promotion, and growth practices are inherently biased in how they are applied. Without addressing these biases, no amount of new hires or workshops will solve the problem; the situation will only perpetuate itself. To create lasting change, leaders must be willing to carefully examine their own behaviors and attitudes, as well as how they design every process and system within the company.

For more Diversity and Inclusion resources, including a free, exhaustive D&I glossary, visit LoveAsABusinessStrategy.com.

THE MANY FACES OF MARGINALIZATION

Have you ever been excluded? Were you ever not invited to a party when everyone else was?

How did that feel?

A marginalized workforce is not only antithetical to a culture of love, but also extremely damaging to business outcomes. The tricky part is, organizations often aren't even aware they are marginalizing their employees. We certainly weren't aware of the extent to which we were marginalizing our Indian team members, but that thoughtlessness created lasting damage to our organization that took us quite a while to repair. Eventually, we understood that, if we wanted to build a culture of love, we needed to actively recognize and attend to the needs and experiences of others, not just ourselves.

Conversations around marginalization usually center around race. While race is important—and while it often *is* a key factor in issues of exclusion and marginalization—it is not the only way a person or a group of people can be marginalized. A person's gender, religion, or ability could also be factors, as well as their job title, wealth, or social status. In fact, whether due to these or other factors, we've all felt excluded or marginalized at different points in our lives— and in both large and small ways.

In order to have discussions around diversity, equity, and inclusion without focusing on any one criterion, it is important to understand the concept of dominant and non-dominant groups. The basic premise of this concept is that, regardless of where you are or what room you enter, some people will have a lot in common in that room and some won't. The former is the dominant group, while the latter is the non-dominant group.

These differences can be subtle, especially when there are obvious similarities among the members of the group. For instance, picture a room full of white men. All of them are married, have two kids, and root for the Packers—and all of them live in a similar type of neighborhood. However, their educational profiles are different; 80 percent of the men went to a private university, while the remaining 20 percent did not.

This difference may not sound as if it would matter that much, but it has the potential to become a constant, subtle undercurrent within many of the group's conversations. For those 20 percent who *didn't* attend a private university, they are constantly reminded of their otherness every time the dominant group starts sharing stories from their college days. It's not that the dominant group means to exclude the other people in the room (just as we didn't mean to exclude our Indian team members). In fact, they're probably not even aware that they're doing it. Nevertheless, this unintentional behavior serves to exclude the non-dominant members—and if this dynamic is left unchecked, it could lead those members to feel like second-tier, or otherwise unequal, team members.

This exclusion is toxic to an organization. It destroys teams, and it hurts team members. When we marginalize people, we communicate through our actions that they are small, diminished, powerless, or otherwise less than the others around them. We push them to the side. Anyone can feel marginalized, and anyone can marginalize.

Marginalization can come in many forms. There are the obvious -isms—sexism, racism, classism, and ageism—but marginalization can happen to anyone for nearly any reason. Some marginalizations are small, and some are really big, extremely harmful ones. Sometimes the worst harm comes from the actions you least consider. In the following sections, we'll offer a few examples to help you better understand the many faces marginalization might take.

CAN'T YOU JUST MAKE DO WITH THESE SCISSORS?

When Frank was fourteen, his dad gave him a new watch for his birthday. He was so excited, he put it on immediately and wore it to school the next day.

Then the kids started asking questions. "Why are you wearing your watch like that? You've got it on the wrong arm."

But Frank didn't have his watch on the wrong arm. He had it on his right arm—his non-dominant arm—just as he had been taught to do. It wasn't that Frank had put his watch on incorrectly; it was that his classmates weren't used to seeing a left-handed person wearing a watch.

If you're part of the 90 percent of the population that is right-handed, you may not think that being left-handed is that big of a deal. But then again, you'd have no reason to notice—the world is literally built for right-handed people like you.

For Frank and other left-handed people, however, navigating a right-handed world is a series of constant compromises and inconveniences. When they write, the text on the pen is upside down, the spine in the notebook gets in their way, and their hand smudges the ink as they move from left to right. If someone is a guitarist or a golfer, their options for testing out equipment at a store are limited or totally nonexistent. Often, they have to special order everything, sight unseen, and hope that the equipment was worth the money. There's more—tape measures are upside down, ergonomic scissors aren't so ergonomic, and can openers are a nightmare.

Aside from these everyday annoyances, Frank has also found that his left-handedness can lead to cultural misunderstandings. For instance, in India your left hand and your right hand are reserved for very specific activities. Your right hand is for eating, and your left hand is for wiping after you've relieved yourself and for putting on or taking off shoes. Frank was aware of this cultural norm before his first visit to India, so he went to great lengths to learn how to eat with his right hand. For the most part, he was successful—but every now and then, he would slip up, grab some food with his left hand, and endure dirty looks.

The experience of being left-handed can feel like a "death by a thousand cuts." Like all left-handers, Frank is able to get through his day just fine. He's even able to have a sense of humor about it (ask him about his "left-handers only" coffee mug that is designed to spill if a righty picks it up—sorry, Candace!). However, being left-handed in a right-handed world means enduring constant, daily inconveniences. It means trying a little bit harder to perform basic tasks. It means planning his activities and purchases in ways that most others aren't accustomed to. And sometimes, it even means eating with his non-dominant hand to avoid offending others.

ONE STRIKE AGAINST YOU

When Chris was growing up, his mom gave Chris and his sister a warning: Chris already had one strike against him because he was Black, and his sister already had two strikes against her because she was both Black and a woman. Then, after explaining the challenges her children would face, Chris's mother would end the conversation with a question: "How many strikes are you going to add before someone takes you out?"

It wasn't an easy thing for Chris and his sister to hear—and it certainly wasn't an easy thing for Chris's mother to say—but she had resolved to prepare her children for an unforgiving world. In many ways, Chris thinks his mother did the right thing. All throughout his formative years, Chris knew that he couldn't afford to make the same mistakes as his peers. The world didn't work the same for people like him—both because he was Black and because his family didn't enjoy high socioeconomic status.

As a result, Chris did what many in marginalized or under-represented groups do in similar situations: he tried to find acceptance through assimilation and overcorrection. As Chris saw it, he didn't have the same margin for error that those in more dominant groups had. He typically felt the need to go along to get along. He didn't want to rock the boat even though he wanted to be accepted and heard for divergent ideas and approaches. Acceptance is a basic human need, but Chris often felt that he had to work harder to get it.

Chris has gained this acceptance, but it has taken a bit of a tradeoff to get there. For instance, when someone asks him to share a moment where he has made a mistake—such as yelling at a teammate or blowing off work—he often is at a loss for words. He doesn't have stories like that because he never felt as if he had access to misbehavior the way those of more dominant groups do before attaining a higher level of authority. The result is that Chris comes off as a perfectionist, or sometimes as unwilling to be vulnerable and admit to past mistakes. So, by trying to play it safe for the sake of being accepted, Chris now must face the fact that his path to leadership may introduce a new strike from some.

THE CHALLENGES OF BEING MUSLIM IN AN AIRPORT

Mohammad is a first-generation immigrant. He was born in Saudi Arabia to Indian parents and moved to the United States when he was sixteen. He is also a practicing Muslim-American and is married to a Russian immigrant. With such a diverse background, Mohammad has found he is judged in different places for different reasons. In India, he often faces judgment for not being Hindu. In America, he is often discriminated against for appearing foreign, even though America has been his home for decades. In Europe, he is all but ignored by restaurant and hotel staff when he dresses casually—but when he dresses like a successful businessman he is given the royal treatment.

There is one place, however, where Mohammad has always been treated the same: airports.

Since the events of September 11, 2001, air travel hasn't been easy for Mohammad. No matter what airport he's in, no matter where he's been or where he's headed, the experience is strikingly similar. First, airlines don't let him check in early online. When he arrives to check in at the counter, his reservation usually has a hold on it—though the agents never seem to know why. Instead, he has to stand around awkwardly for an extra ten to fifteen minutes while the agents not-so-discreetly run a security check.

If that was the extent of his problems, that would still be too much. But it's just the beginning. Mohammad is routinely pulled out of the Security and Immigration line for a secondary investigation. Often, he's pulled out of line right in front of clients, coworkers, or even family, and then he is escorted to a private security room.

Once in these secondary rooms, Mohammad is separated from all his personal belongings—no passport, no phone, no luggage. Sometimes he is asked to remove his clothes and given a full body search, presumably to see if he has any explosives or weapons on him. Then, he is asked a series of questions. "What business are you in?" "Why do you travel?" "What car do you drive?" "Do you have a chemical engineering degree?" Finally, after two or three hours in these glorified holding cells, security thanks him for his cooperation, escorts him out, and tells him to have a nice day.

Two or three hours is a long time to wait. Sometimes, Mohammad is detained ahead of departure, in which case he usually misses his flight. Other times, he is detained after landing, at which point he is tired, hungry, and thirsty from travel. Meanwhile, someone is usually waiting for him outside these holding areas—whether it's his wife and children, another Softway team member, or a client.

During one such detention, Mohammad was passing through New York on his way home from China. He had just been on a flight for fourteen hours straight and had already been waiting in detention for over two and half hours—which caused him to miss his connecting flight. And yet, when he asked for some water, the security officer told him to go drink out of the toilet, further dehumanizing him when he had done nothing wrong.

Mohammad has experienced treatment like this so often that he began to see it as normal. With no other choice, he began to alter his own behaviors just so he could make his flights on time. For instance, at minimum, he would show up at the airport three hours early. And yet, despite these adjustments, there wasn't much he could do to fundamentally change how he was being marginalized. If he wanted to travel, Mohammad had no choice but to comply.

This kind of marginalization is deeply dehumanizing. Every time Mohammad was pulled aside and detained, he was made to feel less valuable than other people, stripped of his humanity and his power, and left without any tools to solve the problem. Such treatment is profoundly wrong, no matter who is experiencing it, or why.

YOU HAVE FELT DIFFERENT TOO

For those of you who aren't left-handed, who aren't Black, or who aren't an Indian Muslim, stories like Frank's, Chris's, or Mohammad's might feel difficult to relate to. However, if you've ever been marginalized, you know at least to some extent what it feels like to be kept out of the conversation. In that way, you don't have to be left-handed to understand what it feels like to be marginalized as a left-handed person. You don't need to be Black to understand what it feels like to be marginalized as a Black person. You don't have to be Muslim to understand what it feels like to be marginalized as a Muslim.

Will your own experiences be a direct one-to-one comparison? Probably not. However, they don't need to be in order for you to gain awareness and empathy for others' struggles. Whoever you are, you have felt different. Whether it came from your upbringing, your education, your family, or the clothes you were wearing, there was a day you walked into a room and were treated differently. When considering issues of marginalization, remember that feeling and use it to inform how you relate to and work to include others.

Creating inclusion in a culture of love is about more than just ensuring that everyone gets a welcome basket during a business trip. It's about more than just rooting out marginalization in all its forms. It's about consciously making room for everyone at the table. It's about how you welcome new team members into the group, how you make everyone feel inside of meetings, and how you handle conflict when it arises. While the work of inclusion isn't accomplished in a day, here are some tips and mindsets to help you along your way.

First, you must understand and accept that differences *do* exist between you and your teammates. Not everyone grows up and experiences life in the same way across the board. Even if you don't know or understand the differences between yourself and a teammate, you *can* understand that they're there. Further, you can understand that those different experiences could bring value and insight that might help the team achieve certain goals.

Second, practice patience. It's not always easy to make room for others whose experiences you don't fully understand. Conflicts, disagreements, and differences are inevitable— but that doesn't mean they need to kill the conversation.

By embracing inclusion, you also embrace the notion that differences are *bridges*, not gaps.

Third, inclusion requires vulnerability. Pride, arrogance, and self-importance are antithetical to a culture of love. In Chapter 6, we'll explore exactly what vulnerability looks like and why it's so important.

Finally, inclusion requires advocacy. This is not a passive process. It's not enough to give people of diverse backgrounds and experiences a seat at the table. You must also make sure they are heard as well. It is every team member's job to elevate the voices of the unheard or the not-included. This means not only rooting out marginalization, but actively building an environment where your coworkers can use their authority, power, and influence. It means, if you are a member of a dominant group, being an ally to help others elevate their voices.

Making certain that everyone has a voice is a critical task. By amplifying and validating the contributions of others who might not otherwise be heard, you not only reinforce the idea that they are welcome and valued, but you help your team develop and vet a broader range of ideas from which to consider and act. This will lead to more discussions, more pushback, and sometimes more conflict; be patient with the process. By hearing more voices, you lessen the risk that everyone together seamlessly runs the business off the proverbial cliff. More perspectives allow for more wisdom.

SELF-AWARENESS IS THE KEY TO INCLUSION

When you're in the dominant group, you're often not aware of it. Because there's little friction in your experience, you aren't aware of the friction that others in a non-dominant group may be experiencing. But if that's the case, how do you fix that?

Once again, the key is to practice introspection in order to bring out better self-awareness. Here are two questions you can ask yourself.

First, who is silent? When the whole group gets together, who is the quietest? By nature, the dominant group is usually the loudest. By identifying the people who aren't speaking up as frequently (if at all), you can work to include them in the group.

Second, whom don't you know on your team? Usually, if you're part of a dominant group, then you likely feel connected to the other members of that group and have solid relationships with them. Therefore, if there is someone you don't know as well, it's probably because they don't share certain traits that you share with the rest of your team.

Once you have a better understanding of who might be feeling marginalized, get active. Have conversations. Use empathy. Pay attention to that team member's individual needs and ask how you can best serve them so that you do not accidentally make a situation worse.

BE THE ALLY

Orienting yourself and your organization around the pillar of inclusion is hard. After all, realizing the problem is only half the battle. Unless you take direct action to solve an instance of marginalization, the problem will only remain—and often grow worse.

To show what we mean, let's return to the opening story of this chapter. Once Chris realized the problem of how our Indian team members were being treated upon arriving in Houston, he had to take several steps to address the issue. First and foremost, he had to help others understand that a problem existed and that it had to be addressed. Unfortunately, when he first brought up the issue to Mohammad, Mohammad pushed back. Softway wasn't treating its Indian team members any differently than any other company would. Why should they go out of their way to change?

The two went back and forth on the issue, with Chris making little headway. Finally, seeing no other option, Chris said he would take on the responsibility himself. If he was the only person who thought it was important to better accommodate their Indian team members, then he would take time out of his personal schedule to do just that.

That's when something finally clicked for Mohammad. Seeing Chris willing to step up and sacrifice his own personal time to help others made Mohammad understand how strongly Chris felt—and how important the issue really was. Just because something is normal, Mohammad realized, that doesn't make it right. Chris wasn't suggesting these changes simply because they were nice things to do. He was trying to correct an injustice that actively hurt their team members. Now that Mohammad was aware of the issue, it wouldn't be right to turn a blind eye to this behavior any longer.

If you see an instance of marginalization and stay silent, then all you do is perpetuate the problem. However, if you have the courage to act, as Chris did, then you can remove marginalization and help to create inclusion and belonging in a powerful way.

Righting the wrongs of marginalization isn't easy. When confronted with injustice, it would be far easier to downplay the problem and say that you didn't mean any harm. But when it comes to marginalization, intention doesn't matter. After all, whether you intend to cause a car accident or not, the result is still the same—and you're still accountable for the aftermath.

Be the voice for those who need to be heard. Acknowledge your harm, and the harm of the organization, and ask yourself how you can be better.

Take responsibility for the impact of your actions. Be willing to examine your own behaviors critically and honestly. Do whatever you can to make it right. If you see a policy that needs to change—or if you see a policy that doesn't yet exist but should—take action.

CHAPTER 5

EMPATHY

Before joining Softway, Chris had never worked for a company with over half of their team members on another continent. At first, interacting with his Indian team members felt strange and new—he couldn't see their faces and had trouble getting a feel for who they were as people. With so much distance in between them, he found it difficult to fully commit to these interactions with his overseas teammates. So, when he began traveling to India to meet with his teammates in person, he was grateful for the opportunity.

During one such trip, Chris had traveled to India with Mohammad. This was a big trip, jam-packed with things to do, meetings to attend, and decisions to make. Chris had almost no downtime—his twenty-hour days were filled to the brim. As busy as he was, Chris soon discovered there was a problem brewing that was far more urgent than anything else on the trip.

One morning before a meeting, Sunil, an HR manager, approached Chris and asked if he could speak with him one-on-one.

"I'm about to step into this meeting, Sunil. Is it urgent?" Chris said.

"Yes," Sunil said. "I *really* need to talk to you today."

Chris could tell by the look on Sunil's face that he was desperate and frustrated. So, Chris agreed to bow out of the meeting and hear what Sunil had to say.

As soon as they found a quiet room to talk, the floodgates opened. Sunil oversaw the HR team in India and had been trying as hard as he could to do right by the company. However, in the eyes of his hiring managers at least, neither he nor his team was succeeding—even worse, the hiring managers would shut him down and tell him to try harder whenever he tried to explain the issue. Not only did Sunil feel as if it had become impossible for him and his team to do their jobs, but that everyone had given up on him—leaders and his peers alike.

Essentially, Sunil was being pulled in two directions. On the one hand, he was tasked with monitoring employee attendance and tracking down any team member who didn't clock in on time. (During this time, Softway was using biometric scanners to monitor employee movement; see Chapter 13 to see just how deep our mistrust ran at the time.). This was a time-consuming task. In fact, it usually took Sunil and his team all morning to call every single late team member and file a report on their whereabouts.

All this time spent tracking down tardy employees meant Sunil and his team had no time to perform their primary job: recruiting new job candidates. So, every day when Sunil came to his afternoon status meeting, he would report that his team was well behind on its quota—which in turn made his managers furious.

Sunil and his team were locked in a vicious cycle. Every day, they spent the morning calling late employees. Every afternoon, they got yelled at. The problem was clearly systemic; Sunil and his teammates had been set up to fail, and it was only a matter of time before they left to find more rewarding work in the competitive Bengaluru job market. Surely someone would treat him better than this.

Chris thanked Sunil for sharing and immediately went and found Mohammad.

"We need to talk, *now*," Chris said.

For the next several minutes, Chris shared everything he'd heard that day—and how deeply it affected him.

JUMP IN THE HOLE

There's an old adage that to understand a person, you must walk a mile in their shoes. After hearing Sunil's story, and many other stories like it, Chris gained a profound sense of empathy for his Indian teammates, and he resolved to do something about it.

It's not easy to fully understand and embrace a situation that someone else is going through. Doing so requires not only a high level of emotional intelligence, but also a willingness to bear the same burden someone else might be experiencing. It is for these reasons that practicing empathy may be the most challenging Pillar of Love—and also the most critical.

As one of our colleagues says, "Empathy is being able to turn off your mic and turn up the volume on everyone else." In other words, empathy is about not just listening to the needs of others, but also seeking to understand their emotional experience. Empathy asks, "When have I dealt with something similar? What would this feel like?" By recognizing the feeling that someone is going through, you are feeling that feeling with them. Then, working from that shared perspective, empathy is the act of moving forward together with that person rather than leaving them to struggle on their own.

So what does empathy look like in a culture of love? We've found that empathy is best understood through a concept known as *empathetic leadership*. We'll explain what that means in a moment. But to get there, first we need to draw a little contrast and show you what leadership—or, should we say *management*—looks like without empathy.

> Empathy means understanding and sharing the emotional experience that someone else is having.

THE APATHETIC MANAGER

Imagine you've just fallen into a big hole. After you spend a few minutes shouting for help, eventually someone comes along.

"What are you doing down in that hole?" the person says. "Get out—there's work to do!"

This is essentially what Sunil's managers were saying to him every time he spent the morning putting out fires and putting off his recruiting calls. They refused to see that Sunil and his team were struggling, and so they did little to help them. Sunil's managers were apathetic to his situation.

You can spot apathetic managers from a mile away; they're the ones who always demand that you put your feelings aside and get your work done. It's not that they have no feelings, but rather that they believe pushing those feelings aside is an appropriate way to lead in a business.

Needless to say, the apathetic manager has no place in a culture of love. By focusing only on outcomes, Sunil's managers were effectively ignoring his humanity and leaving him to fend for himself. This insistence on quotas might have worked in the short term, but as Sunil made all too clear when he explained his situation to Chris, in the long term it had only led to much bigger problems within the organization.

THE SYMPATHETIC MANAGER

You're still in the hole, and you're still trying to figure a way out. Eventually, someone else comes along and sees your predicament.

"I'm so sorry you're in that hole," this new person says. "That must be terrible!" Then, they too continue on their way.

Well, at least that person was more pleasant, you think to yourself. But the result is the same. You're still in the hole.

This is the inherent challenge of working with a sympathetic manager. Sure, they mean well, but they rarely offer support in a way that empowers team members and furthers their growth.

Typically, the sympathetic manager responds to their team members' problems in one of two ways. First, there's the over-helpful approach. If your parents ever finished your homework for you when you were struggling, then you've seen the over-helpful approach in action. In the workplace, you've seen the over-helpful approach any time a manager has pulled you off a job in order to "take the burden off of you." Sure, they were coming from a place of goodness, but instead of creating opportunities for growth, the sympathetic manager just redistributes the burden to others.

Just as destructive as the over-helpful approach is the hands-tied approach. "I'm sorry that's happening to you," the sympathetic manager might say, "but there's nothing I can do to help."

When Chris first heard Sunil's story, his initial response skirted this line. He was horrified by what he heard, but uncertain of what he could do other than to assure Sunil that his concerns were heard and understood. If all Chris had done was listen, it would have given Sunil some sense of psychological safety, but it would have done little else. The HR nightmare would still exist, and Sunil and his team would be no better off than they were before.

Fortunately, Chris didn't stop there. The more he heard stories like Sunil's, the more he realized something *had* to be done—or else the problem would only compound.

Okay, one more time. You're back in the hole, and things still aren't going well. Once again, someone walks by. But this time, the moment this person sees your predicament, they jump into the hole with you.

"All right," the person says, "let's get out of here. How can I help?"

That's what empathy—and empathetic leadership—looks like.

Throughout this discussion, you may have noticed that we've been careful to distinguish between the terms *manager* and *leader*. While these terms are often used interchangeably, to us their respective meanings are worlds apart.

Managers are people with formal authority and position. They oversee other team members, but they don't lead them. Further, managers could exist at the very highest levels of a company. You could be the VP of an entire division and enjoy all the authoritative power that comes with it, but you might still only be a manager.

Leaders, on the other hand, serve their team members by supporting, mentoring, coaching, and otherwise setting their teams up for success. Leadership is learned—and ultimately earned—on the job. A leader earns the title, not through a formal promotion, but when their fellow team members choose to follow them.

For Chris, leading from a place of empathy enabled him to create a supportive space for Sunil, to find a way forward, and to leave everyone better off than they were before.

He took action as a leader to address the situation. However, as we'll explain in greater detail in Chapter 6, just getting to this point required vulnerability. If Sunil hadn't been vulnerable and shared his struggles with a VP (which must have been terrifying), Chris wouldn't have been able to support Sunil as an empathetic leader. Similarly, if Chris hadn't been practicing vulnerability as well, he may not have been compelled to take action. Fortunately, he did.

To address the problem, first Chris brought Mohammad into the conversation, putting him face-to-face with Sunil so that he could hear Sunil's story firsthand. This not only brought visibility to the issue, but it allowed Mohammad to make the same empathetic connection that Chris had. Then, Chris and Mohammad resolved to change HR's approach to recruiting—specifically, to eliminate arbitrary quotas. Finally, over the next several weeks, they designed new training for the management team in India, so that they would be more aligned with their team members and be better able to reach the outcomes they so badly wanted.

The result? Recruiting was completely overhauled, Sunil could enjoy work again, and Softway became more effective at recruiting and retention. But more importantly, Chris's display of empathy created an unshakeable bond between him, Sunil, and the company at large. As Sunil, who is still with the company, told us as we interviewed him for this story, "Everything good about me I learned at Softway and everything bad about me, is just me."

What a difference.

Apathetic management takes care of the business while disregarding the person. Sympathetic management takes care of the person while disregarding the business. Empathetic leadership takes care of the person in the context of the business.

THE KEY TRAITS OF EMPATHY

How do you become an empathetic leader? The most important requirement for empathy is emotional intelligence. This means being able to read the situation, assume good intent no matter how others are behaving, and connect your own experience to theirs in a way that leads to understanding.

One way to build emotional intelligence is to practice empathetic listening, in which you tune out everything else and focus directly on the other person. By listening to what the person is actually saying, rather than only hearing what you want to hear, you can respond to that person's needs productively. Empathetic listening takes practice. It can be difficult to both hear what the person is saying and ask yourself where you might have had a similar experience or feeling. It sometimes requires imagination. You may not be a parent, for instance, so it may be hard for you to understand some of the challenges of being a parent. However, with effort, you can likely pull out some commonalities from your own experience.

The work of empathy requires practice and participation—and because of that, you're going to feel uncomfortable from time to time. Sometimes you may not realize that you have more listening to do, and other times you may be unsure which questions to ask. That's all part of the learning process. Be patient, practice introspection, and apply your learning to your next interaction.

THE GOLDEN RULE VS. THE PLATINUM RULE

Everyone has heard of the Golden Rule: treat others as you would want to be treated yourself. The rule might sound pretty good on paper, but in practice, the Golden Rule can get you into trouble, since it asks you to assume a lot. In essence, every time you apply the Golden Rule, you're saying, "I assume you should be treated in accordance with my worldview and how I was raised. I will treat you based on my own experiences, rather than your own." Sure you may have good intentions, but in retrospect, doesn't that approach sound a little selfish?

Instead of the Golden Rule, we're big believers in the Platinum Rule: treat others as they would want to be treated. When you show empathy for their own perspective and experiences, you will be better able to help them.

As with most empathetic practices, the Platinum Rule requires some more work than the Golden Rule. After all, it's practically impossible to treat someone how they'd like to be treated without first getting to know them; learning about their habits, perspectives, and experiences; and trying to feel how they are feeling. Further, the Platinum Rule can't easily be scaled. It requires approaching people on an individual level to try and see the world through their own unique lens.

Sometimes, moving organizational goals forward means getting buy-in from a person with whom you may very well not agree. In such a situation, having a strong sense of empathy—and treating them how they want to be treated—will get you further toward your own desired outcomes.

In that way, the Platinum Rule helps you practice empathy even for people who challenge you. Just remember, in such situations, it's your job to use empathy and create space for everyone in the room, not just one person. One person may require a lot of attention, but everyone deserves to be heard and understood. The Platinum Rule must be applied fairly.

GET WALKIN'

Now that you understand the value of empathy to an organization and what empathetic leadership looks like, you may be wondering: What happened to Sunil and the rest of the Bengaluru HR team?

We want to wrap this chapter by telling you the story of how we came to solve India's HR quagmire. After all, empathy isn't just hearing someone's problems and telling them you feel bad for them—that's sympathy. Instead, empathy is about taking action.

To understand how we arrived at our solution, we need to backtrack a bit—back to the early days of our culture of love. Before our pivot, Mohammad practiced what we call "management by bossing around." Instead of getting out and interacting with his team members, he mostly sat in his office and told people what to do. The more the company was in trouble, the more he would create processes and tools for people to follow. As a result, Mohammad set up a number of unrealistic expectations: five contracts a day, ten proposals, a full-fledged project plan in two days.

If you're seeing a parallel between Mohammad's misbehaviors and those of Sunil's managers, that's no mistake. Because Mohammad didn't have a strong concept of what his team members' day-to-day reality was, and because he made no effort to find out—he had no idea how unrealistic his expectations were. When people struggled—as they inevitably did—Mohammad didn't show compassion, but rather annoyance.

As we were transitioning into a culture of love, Mohammad realized there was a lot about how the company and his team members operated that he didn't know. He quickly set out to change that by experiencing a few roles within the company firsthand. First, he served as a project manager, then as a salesperson, then as a technologist, and then—for a brief and frustrating five minutes—as a creative.

In each of the roles, Mohammad encountered unrealistic

goals, which led to unintended pressure, which led to inevitable consequences and endless stress. He experienced the processes, rules, and structures he alone had made for each role—and he didn't like those experiences one bit. He had been asking his team to do things that he himself could not deliver.

But while it was a frustrating experiment, it was also an eye-opening one. Mohammad realized the kind of pressure he had put his team under and the impossible tasks he had asked of them. Rather than helping them become more efficient, his systems and processes had set unrealistic expectations and inhibited their ability to perform. He wasn't empowering his teams; he was holding them back.

As soon as he realized this, Mohammad developed a new appreciation for his team members and their day-to-day reality. From that day on, he vowed that before he decided to just roll out a shiny new process, procedure, or policy, he needed to see it in action. He needed to experiment to ensure that he wasn't asking anyone to do anything that he couldn't do. Then he needed to ask others to do the same and offer their feedback. Through this process, Mohammad found new empathy, and empathy made him a better leader.

Flash forward a few months later. Mohammad is in the Bengaluru office with Chris. He has just heard of the massive issue confronting HR and their recruiting processes, and he knows exactly what to do: let the hiring managers walk a mile in Sunil's shoes.

For the next several weeks, Mohammad and Chris set out to retrain all the hiring managers in Bengaluru's HR department. Through a series of exercises, the managers were placed in the exact same situation as Sunil and his team-mates—same job, same circumstances, same objectives, same timeline. Mohammad and Chris watched as, one by one, the hiring managers each came to the same realization as Sunil: there is simply no way they can get all this work done and still reach their goals on time. What these managers had thought was an easy task was actually an impossible one.

At the end of the exercise, many of the managers responded in the same way. They walked right up to their direct reports and immediately apologized.

At that moment, they were no longer managers. They were leaders in the making.

LESS FRICTION, BETTER RESULTS

Inside of every team, every division, and every company, people are different from one another—and this is a good thing. A company that is built out of a variety of people of dif-ferent backgrounds, ethnicities, and skillsets becomes greater than any one individual. However, the same differences that ultimately lead to strength and innovation can also cause friction between people if we are not careful. That's where empathy comes in.

Empathy naturally creates connections, and its use over time builds cultural competence. Using empathy teaches you to more easily negotiate differences and connect with others from your similarities. You become able to foster inclusion. Empathy bridges gaps across geographical and company cultures, and bridges gaps between team members with differing personalities. It smooths out conflict. It builds strong, resilient relationships.

Empathy builds real connections between people and allows difference to deliver tremendous value to the organization. However, it's not a free ride.

To see the gains of empathy, leaders must do the work to relate to every team member, without any of the group being excluded, often translating one team member's experience to another. If you can do that, if you can be empathetic to the needs of your various team members and provide the tools, resources, and mentoring they need, the result is magic. You foster a space where people genuinely care for one another and feel empowered. You build dynamic, high-performing teams.

Teams must also practice empathy between themselves consistently to see results. When they do, they build better relationships with each other, but also with customers and clients. This in turn leads to better-developed products and services that truly address customer needs. As a result, customers spend more and stay more loyal. Furthermore, a deep understanding of customers leads directly to new revenue opportunities you might otherwise not have found.

Empathy reduces team attrition and builds team loyalty. People who are treated with empathy feel a sense of belonging, a sense that their work matters and that their leaders and coworkers care about them. This in turn leads them to engage more actively with their teammates, forging deeper long-term bonds.

Empathy—like our next couple pillars, vulnerability and

trust—works in a positively reinforcing cycle. In other words, the greatest byproduct of empathy is more empathy. However, just like with vulnerability and trust, building empathy into your culture of love is going to require a leap of faith—which means that, as a leader, you have to be willing to go first.

CHAPTER 6

VULNERABILITY

Things weren't going well in the project management department. Every day, Jeff found himself amazed at the dysfunction, mistakes, and overall lack of accountability his project managers displayed. Jeff was astounded that even one person could be so incompetent, let alone a whole team.

It was a big mess—Jeff's mess—and he wasn't sure how to fix it. He wasn't even sure where to start.

So, he struck a "cool boss" pose and implemented an open-door policy. His team members would be autonomous, but if anyone had questions or needed help, all they had to do was pop into his office and ask. No problem was too small. No question too dumb. He was there if they needed him.

Apparently, no one ever needed him. Not a single project manager ever came through his door to ask for help. Guess he wasn't *that* cool after all.

This irritated Jeff to no end. His team was struggling at every turn. They were making mistakes that were so baffling and so counterintuitive that it made his head spin. And yet no one sought his assistance. To Jeff, it was painfully obvious how badly they needed him—so why couldn't they get out of their own ways and come seek his boundless wisdom?

Eventually, after a lot of introspection, Jeff had an epiphany: the project managers couldn't see the problem because they weren't the problem. They weren't the ones making mind-bogglingly bad mistakes. Jeff was.

An open-door policy isn't about the door, but about the person. When Jeff first instituted the policy, his project managers *did* come to him with problems. However, they quickly learned that Jeff himself was anything but an open door. Not only was he regularly dismissive of his project managers' problems, but he was also generally unwilling to do anything about them, preferring to give advice from on high and let them sort the details out. Jeff's door may have been open, but Jeff himself was unapproachable, intimidating, and distant.

Struggling with an underperforming team, Jeff responded as an apathetic manager rather than as an empathetic leader. His open-door policy was nothing more than an attempt to disassociate from the problem so he wouldn't have to deal with it. That way, he could tell himself that his project managers' problems were their own and not his. If they couldn't shape up, that was on them.

By this point, Jeff had a good sense of the real problem (himself), but he wanted to understand just how bad it was. So, he began asking around, both inside and outside the department, for honest feedback about his performance as a leader. The feedback he received confirmed his fears—and then some. In fact, as he learned from Mohammad, the situation was worse than he'd thought. His project managers would vent to each other behind Jeff's back. They'd go over Jeff's head to complain to Mohammad about the problems in their department. They were fed up with Jeff and his open-door policy, and if things didn't change soon, he was going to lose a lot of good people.

Jeff may have sought this feedback out, but that didn't make it any easier to process. After listening to Mohammad, he took time to digest the feedback. Finally, he understood the full scope of the problem—and he was ready to change. To do that, he knew he had to do something that made him deeply uncomfortable: he had to get vulnerable with his team.

PERMISSION TO BE HUMAN

Vulnerability, our third Pillar of Love, isn't always easy. It takes a lot of courage—one more time for the folks in the back—*a lot* of courage, but it's almost always worth it. In fact, we'd go so far as to say it's the secret sauce of building human relationships; when people see you being vulnerable, they want to be more vulnerable too.

Jeff knew that if he was going to re-establish trust with his team, he was going to have to get more vulnerable than he'd ever been in his professional life. First, he scheduled a series of one-on-ones with every single team member. Each meeting began the same—with an apology. "First of all, I'd like to apologize for the type of leader I've been," Jeff said. "I'm just now realizing the harm it has caused, and I would like to take some time to explain how I view that failure." From there, Jeff would describe the specific harm his behaviors caused to that particular person. Afterward, he shared where he was in his journey as a leader, the revelation he had recently experienced, and what he intended to do about it.

Jeff wasn't just showing vulnerability with his team members. By opening up, he was also making a commitment to build trust with his team—and inviting them to do the same. From that point onward, the very nature of his meetings and one-on-ones changed. Instead of talking about work and deliverables, they focused on building relationships.

The more these relationships grew, the more their empathy for each other grew as well. No longer did Jeff's project managers talk about his failings behind his back—and no longer did Jeff reflexively blame his project managers for every little thing that went wrong. Over time, not only did project management grow into a high-performing team, but Jeff grew into a high-performing leader. And through that transformation, he learned a valuable lesson: it's hard to be an apathetic leader when you understand and care about your team members.

This was a hard-won lesson. After all, it takes a lot of mental energy to hold onto unforgiveness, to get caught up in office politics, to tiptoe around your manager so you can deliver bad news gently. It takes far less energy to simply share how you're feeling and move on. Now that the issue was out in the open, Jeff had regained the trust and empathy of his team—and in so doing, freed up their mental energy to focus on their work, rather than on office drama. Sure, there were still some big problems to solve. But now the project managers knew Jeff had their back; they were ready to look beyond Jeff's failure, dig in, and get to the root of those problems.

A culture rooted in vulnerability allows people to be open and honest and share meaningful emotions. It means we're willing to own mistakes and to learn from those mistakes, rather than having to be seen as perfect.

A WOLF IN VULNERABILITY CLOTHING

Vulnerability gets a bad rap in the workplace. In fact, it's often seen as a weakness. Many of us are taught to wall off our personal selves—the people we are at home—and to show up only as our professional selves. That's ultimately to the detriment of everyone. When we are willing to be imperfect, we can move on from our struggles and issues much faster.

But where does this resistance to vulnerability come from? Simply put, it's because we've all been burned by being vulnerable at one point or another, and that feeling can be tough to let go of. Think about it for a moment: have you ever experienced a conversation with someone who assumed the guise of vulnerability either to seek pity or to make someone else feel guilty? Rather than sharing out of a sense of empathy and authenticity, this was merely manipulating the situation to their own end.

This is not what we mean when we talk about vulnerability. In fact, this behavior is the antithesis of vulnerability. Sharing for the sake of manipulation is known as floodlighting—or deliberately obscuring the facts of a situation to confuse others and get what you want. Such behavior is toxic to a culture of love.

EVERYDAY VULNERABILITY

Vulnerability in the workplace isn't all about sharing your emotions, admitting to your mistakes, and describing your deepest, darkest secrets. Vulnerability can also be expressed by sharing your emotional state and your current situation with others. In fact, often vulnerability is as simple as saying, "I'm sorry, I'm not in a good headspace right now. Can you handle this so I can take some time to decompress?"

Mohammad in particular has become well-known for this

kind of pragmatic, everyday vulnerability. One day, for instance, Mohammad arrived at a meeting feeling out of sorts. Earlier that day, someone had broken his trust—and they had done so in a way that not only injured his sense of honor, but that raised important legal questions.

With so much weighing on Mohammad's mind, he found himself distracted and angry on a call with Jeff, Chris, and Frank. Before Softway adopted its Six Pillars of Love, the old Mohammad would have tried to power through the meeting with a chip on his shoulder, allowing the actions of others to cause him to misbehave. The new Mohammad had the self-awareness to be vulnerable with the rest of his team instead. When he shared his problem and asked for a little space to clear his head, Jeff, Chris, and Frank were more than happy to oblige.

In the team's eyes, it wasn't just a matter of giving Mohammad space. They knew that they were part of Mohammad's support structure, and at that moment, he was asking for help. It was clear how much the problem was weighing on him, especially after he chose to cancel several other calls later on that day. Seeing this, Jeff, Chris, and Frank didn't just create space for Mohammad to process his feelings, but they also checked in with him to offer their support and see if there was anything else they could do.

Many CEOs wouldn't have felt they could show emotions like that, much less walk away from their work for a day. However, by making this decision, Mohammad not only took care of himself, but also his team, which no longer was at risk of dealing with the emotional blowback of Mohammad's situation. Better still, this show of vulnerability reinforced the trust and empathy he had placed in his team and showcased the right behaviors for them to emulate. By transparently sharing that he was struggling, Mohammad invited the team to get to know him more deeply, and to enthusiastically offer him the support he needed.

It's always difficult to share the struggle at the time. However, we've all found that as soon as we have shared it, weight comes off our shoulders. By creating an environment for others to have empathy toward you, you also create a support system of people who want to help get you out of whatever hole you find yourself in. If you don't do that, you close yourself off to that support—never even realizing it was available in the first place. After all, it's hard for others to be empathetic toward your situation if you don't share your situation in the first place.

That's what vulnerability is all about. It may not change the situation, but it *does* contribute to feelings of safety, understanding, and resilience. When Mohammad arrived at his next set of meetings the next day, he was engaged, warm, and grateful for the opportunity to clear his head.

IT'S OKAY TO BE UNCERTAIN

At his previous job, Chris witnessed a moment of vulnerability that completely altered his relationship to problem-solving. At the time he was working for a woman who presented a tough, unimpeachable front 99 percent of the time. One day, however, as they were working through a tough challenge, she let her guard down. "If I'm being honest," she said, "I have no idea how to figure this situation out."

For one fleeting moment, it was as if the mask had slipped and Chris could see who this person really was. And the experience has stuck with him ever since. Suddenly, Chris understood that no one had all the answers—not even the people he deeply admired. From that moment onward, he began approaching every problem with a new mindset. It wasn't about having all the answers, but about figuring those answers out! If the road to finding those answers was messy and uncertain, it didn't matter. He knew that by sharing with others and being transparent about his process, he could get there.

A PRACTICE OF RENEWAL

Vulnerability doesn't happen by accident. You don't wake up one day, flip a switch, and suddenly become vulnerable. Among other things, it requires attention, authenticity, humility, and active engagement with others.

For Jeff, admitting his shortcomings to his team took a great deal of humility. But so did reaching out to others and actively seeking feedback—even if that meant hearing some hard truths. In doing so, he gave himself the opportunity to truly hear the feedback, to form a plan of change, and to begin to work on solving the problem. Since that initial breakthrough, Jeff has made active feedback a regular part of his development, inviting others into his journey to becoming a better leader.

Not only is this good for Jeff, but the practice is contagious.

When project managers see Jeff actively seeking opportunities to improve, they can't help but want to do the same. When they see Jeff owning up to a mistake he has made, they understand they have permission to make their own mistakes as well.

To create that kind of space within your own team, here are a few bits of advice.

First, let go of ego, and drop the fear of failure. It's easy to get caught up in this idea that we have to be invincible and that we must never fail—and when we do fail, we can't show weakness by admitting it for fear of being judged. This mindset is rampant not only in the business world, but in our society at large. Unfortunately, this mindset isn't doing us any good.

Here's the truth: Your job isn't to be perfect all the time. Your job is to bring your ideas to the table and to create a successful organization. In our experience, a successful organization is nothing but a series of mistakes that turned into opportunities. Viewed from that lens, vulnerability is a sign of strength, not a sign of weakness. If you shy away from that strength rather than embrace it, then you risk missing out on the very opportunities that could propel your organization forward.

Second, don't be mean. Vulnerability is not an excuse to express yourself in a way that hurts others or threatens their psychological safety. While vulnerability is absolutely an exercise in being your true, authentic self, it's also about being your *best* self—which shouldn't require being needlessly blunt, rude, or destructive to others. The point of vulnerability is understanding, learning, and growth. The experience should positively impact you and those around you, not leave them feeling like trash.

When applied correctly, vulnerability promotes a sense of psychological safety. We work better when we know we have permission to be uncertain, to make mistakes, and to take ownership of those mistakes without ridicule or blame. It's no surprise, then, that vulnerable teams are high-performing teams. Teams operating in a psychologically safe environment communicate better, solve problems more effectively, and are more creative and innovative.

That makes sense. If you know you can mess up and be heard fairly, you don't have to waste time on unnecessary bureaucracy. You avoid wasted days and weeks of worry. You proceed confidently knowing you have opportunities to fix mistakes and move on. Most important of all, you know you have permission to take risks, try something new, and embrace the results whether things work out perfectly or not.

This is precisely what happened to Jeff and his project management team. It took time for Jeff to build new working relationships with each of his project managers. It took a lot of active listening to understand his PMs' struggles and respond with empathy. It even required Jeff to sit in on several client meetings to better understand the nuances of the project manager role and how he could better facilitate it.

None of this would have worked if the team suspected for a moment that Jeff wasn't committed to them. They had to hear him say he'd never dealt with clients on the level that they had, and that he had never managed projects the way they had. They had to see him go to client meetings and learn to manage a project. They had to see him admit what he didn't know and respond with empathy to them. They had to see him show up day by day, earning credibility.

But once they see that, the results speak for themselves. These days, the project management team is one of the strongest at Softway. Mohammad calls them his "mini-CEOs" and regularly recruits from that team for senior leadership roles (see Chapter 14). He credits the newfound strength of the project management team to Jeff—and specifically, to Jeff's willingness to be vulnerable and commit to change.

For his part, Jeff isn't ready to take all the credit for this transformation. However, he has seen the difference in the close relationships he has built with his project managers, and in the way they're quick to come to him with questions or problems. Jeff's cool-boss, open-door policy days may be over, but now his team knows—they *trust*—that he is always there to listen and lend a hand. But it goes deeper than that. Practicing vulnerability has fundamentally changed the way Jeff views and engages in his personal and professional relationships. Because he is vulnerable with others, they have in turn been vulnerable with him, forging bonds that extend far beyond the workplace. As Jeff says, he would trust many of his fellow team members with his life.

Leadership in a culture of love is being vulnerable in the face of struggle and taking ownership for your part in that struggle. It's saying you don't know everything, but you want to work with the team. You're committed to working with them.

It's simple, but it takes tremendous courage. After all, it's not easy to let your guard down. It's not easy to admit that you aren't perfect. It's not easy to take off the armor you've put on as a result of previous experiences, relationships, and workplaces—and to stop pretending to be invincible. But the more you do it, the more you give permission to others to do it as well.

CHAPTER 7

TRUST

Frank does not have a four-year degree. There, we said it.

He could have pursued a degree, but he opted out of getting one. Instead, after he had earned an associate's degree at a community college, his dad invited him to join a startup he had founded—and he leapt at the chance. Joining his dad's technology company turned out to be one of the best decisions he ever made (and as a result of his father's sudden death at fifty, when Frank was just twenty-six, it also ended up being a precious few years spent together). Joining a startup at such a young age taught Frank some incredible lessons that he likely wouldn't have learned through more traditional education.

Joining his dad's company is also how Frank came to learn about Softway, because his dad was an early client. Through his work for Softway and other organizations, Frank saw another new business opportunity—so, in true entrepreneurial fashion, he co-created another company to pursue. Then, just four months after incorporating his new company, he sold it to Softway and joined our leadership team.

All this good fortune likely wouldn't have happened if Frank had chosen to follow a traditional path, and he is proud of all that he has accomplished and where he has ended up. But even to this day, he is sensitive about the fact that he doesn't have an advanced degree.

In fact, you could say that Frank exhibits all the classic signs of impostor syndrome. When everyone around him has an advanced degree (some with two, three, or more), he can't help but feel like the odd person out. Frank knows that he's been successful, and yet he constantly questions his career path. Worse, he fears that one day he will be outed by his peers as a bona fide imposter—not invited to meetings, shunned around the water cooler (or in his case, more likely the espresso machine), and otherwise treated as fundamentally less-than when compared to the rest of his teammates.

To compensate for this crippling fear of being found out, Frank adopted some unique behaviors over the years. Sometimes, he would just shut down. For instance, if he was in a group of people and they were speaking negatively about people who didn't have college degrees—not knowing that Frank was one of those people—Frank would fall silent, look down at the floor, and then walk away. Other times, especially when he was meeting with a high-profile client, Frank would prepare to lie about his degree and where he earned it, just in case. He would even research professors at the school just in case he needed to elaborate on his experience. Fortunately, he never had to pull that card.

This may sound like extreme behavior, but from Frank's point of view, he was doing his part to protect Softway. Many of the clients and decision-makers had multiple advanced degrees—

some even had doctorates. Frank was certain that if he was found out, none of these people would want to do business with him or the company anymore.

Eventually, Frank realized he couldn't go on feeling this way forever. So one day, in the spirit of bringing his full self to work, he decided to open up about his educational background. This was a big leap for Frank, and he wasn't sure how it was going to turn out. But rather than fear what he couldn't control, Frank chose to trust that his teammates would lift him up rather than tear him down.

One of the first people Frank confided in was Jeff. By this time, Frank and Jeff had been working together on projects for years—ranging from high-end consulting with Softway's most prestigious clients, to short-form comedy sketches only seen on Snapchat. To Frank, Jeff had become not only a coworker, but also a friend. And since he held a bachelor's degree himself, Jeff was also the type of person Frank feared might judge him. Despite their history together, opening up to Jeff felt like a leap of faith.

But when Jeff heard Frank's story, he just shrugged.

"That's it?" Jeff said. "I don't care about any of that, man. You're still Frank. You're still the person I know and love and care about."

This was exactly the response Frank was hoping for. In fact, the more he introspected on that conversation, the more he realized how much he had needed validation for his choices— especially from someone like Jeff, whom he trusted and admired. He needed to know that his teammates accepted him for who he was, not for the number of degrees he did or didn't hold.

The more Frank shared, the more he found that most of his teammates responded just like Jeff. Frank felt as if he was revealing some big secret, but their reactions made it clear that Frank did, in fact, belong. His work and work ethic spoke more to his ability than a four-year degree. His teammates listened to his story and accepted him for who he was.

As he heard his teammates' acceptance, something changed in Frank. The impostor syndrome didn't disappear completely, but it did shrink down to a much more manageable size. Jeff, or any of the rest of Frank's teammates, could have used this knowledge against him. Instead, they responded with empathy, thanked him for sharing, and reaffirmed their personal and professional bonds with him.

Stories like this highlight why trust is one of our Six Pillars of Love. When we trust our teammates, we have confidence in them, in their integrity, strength, and ability to perform a difficult task, manage a responsibility, and, as in Frank's case, maintain psychological safety. It's not easy to open up to someone and share a part of yourself that could be used against you. In a culture of love, trust should always be rewarded. But to do that, we must learn to push beyond superficial forms of trust and work toward something deeper.

THE TWO KINDS OF TRUST

Usually, when we think of trust, we think of *predictive trust*. Predictive trust is based on the idea that you know someone well enough to predict what they may think or do.

You've seen them in action for a long time, or you're close to them in some way, and so you trust them because you can predict how they will act. You trust that Mohammad will be eager to talk about the most recent University of Houston game. You trust that Chris will find a way to work a Beyoncé reference into the conversation. You trust that Frank will brew a perfect cup of coffee with his trusty Hario V60 before the next meeting starts. You trust that Jeff will break out one of his many, many board games whenever you're over for a dinner party. Predictive trust is stable, but also superficial. It's based on patterns and perception, not on relationships.

When Frank began sharing his story with his teammates, a small group of bad actors responded to this information with jealousy and anger, and they began to actively undermine and marginalize Frank from that point on.

This is the problem with predictive trust: it limits a person only to a specific aspect of who they are and what they have done in the past.

During meetings, these teammates became uninterested in Frank's feedback because—as they stated in their own words— they believed he wasn't qualified to have an opinion. Further, they were unwilling to trust Frank with new responsibilities. If he hadn't done something before (or because he didn't have a piece of paper that said he could do it), then they didn't believe he was capable.

In that way, predictive trust really isn't trust at all—at least, not the kind of trust that leads to growth. And because certain members of Frank's team operated from such a narrow band of knowledge, the group as a whole was unable to collaborate, innovate, and grow.

After this had gone on for a while, Frank decided that he was tired of being marginalized because of his education. He was tired of the verbal attacks, tired of the emotional abuse, and tired of being blocked out of important decisions for what he saw as an arbitrary reason. So, one night during a trip to San Francisco, Frank shared his story with Chris and what he had been experiencing as a result.

Immediately, this got Chris thinking differently about his friend and teammate—specifically, how much more he could do to include Frank at the table. It's easy to make an offhand reference to the old college—to dorm life, to tailgate parties, to the feeling of pulling an all-nighter for a big exam. These stories work because they're good at forging connections with others—so long as everyone has had the same shared experiences and followed a similar educational path.

Now that Chris knew Frank *didn't* share those experiences, he got to thinking about all the times he had unintentionally marginalized Frank through these offhand references. Considering the insecurity Frank felt about his education, and considering that some at Softway had actively weaponized this perceived difference, Chris was grateful that Frank had confided in him.

Through this exchange, Chris and Frank formed a deeper trust—what is known as *vulnerability-based trust*. Vulnerability-based trust is built out of what the *Harvard Business Review* refers to as the three elements of trust: relationships, expertise, and consistency. Each element is important, but relationships are ultimately the determining factor in building vulnerability-based trust. If a person is inconsistent or lacks crucial expertise, trust in that person might take a hit, but it can be rebuilt. If a person betrays a relationship, however, it may be impossible for others to ever trust in them again.[3]

Through the lens of vulnerability-based trust, the fact that Frank didn't have an advanced degree didn't matter— Mohammad knew Frank's education when he hired him, and he didn't care. What he also knew was that Frank had both the expertise and the consistency to contribute to the company, to think creatively, and to deliver excellent service to Softway's clients. Over the next several years, Mohammad, Jeff, and Chris saw Frank deliver time and time again, and they knew they could predict with relative certainty that he would continue to do so. This is the power of empowerment at play (which we'll be digging into in the next chapter).

However, because they also had a strong foundational relationship with Frank, their trust extended further. When leaders operate from a place of vulnerability-based trust with their team members, they empower those people to go beyond their skillsets. They are willing to allow their teams to operate with uncertainty, risk, and emotional exposure because they know a fundamental secret of human nature: the more you practice vulnerability-based trust with others, the more they will reward that trust through exemplary effort. This is the kind of trust that allowed our project managers to shine under tremendous pressure (see the next chapter), and this is the kind of trust Mohammad placed in Frank.

---

3 Jack Zenger and Joseph Folkman. "The 3 Elements of Trust." *Harvard Business Review.* February 5, 2019. https://hbr.org/2019/02/the-3-elements-of-trust

Unfortunately, certain members of Frank's team didn't have this same kind of vulnerable trust. So, when they saw Mohammad or others giving Frank new responsibilities, they openly revolted. "I spent a lot of money to get my degree," one team member told Mohammad, "and Frank thinks he can tell *me* what to do?"

To be clear, such mindsets and misbehaviors weren't compatible with a culture of love, and ultimately neither were the leaders who exhibited them (see Chapter 14). But, ultimately, their objections were meaningless when Frank consistently rose to—and often exceeded—every challenge placed in front of him.

When teams operate from a place of predictive trust, they see their work only in terms of what they know, rather than what is *possible*. They're reluctant to experiment, to explore, or otherwise to take risks. Worse, they're reluctant to encourage that behavior in others. They don't trust what they don't know, and therefore their trajectory is limited. They never grow.

This is where it's crucial for leaders to set the example, as Mohammad did with Frank. The spell of predictive trust can be broken, and anyone can learn to practice vulnerability-based trust. But the change has to start at the top.

WHERE'S THE TRUST?

Leadership without trust isn't leadership at all—it's management. Often, we don't recognize that there is a trust deficit until it's too late: either a team has wasted massive amounts of time and energy, or it has failed altogether.

To avoid such an outcome, leaders must be willing to both trust and be trusted. Further, they must be able to forgive and ask for forgiveness. These are the signs of true servant leadership (see Chapters 9 and 10).

HOW TO TAKE A LEAP OF FAITH (AND STICK THE LANDING)

Ask the members of a team broadly whether they trust each other, and they'll invariably say yes. However, ask a few more targeted questions, and things start to get more interesting:

> How often do you give each other feedback?

> How do you handle mistakes?

> Are you willing to talk to a coworker directly and plainly about their mistake even if it hurts their feelings? Or, do you beat around the bush?

Questions like this often get to the heart of the matter—often revealing that a team's trust is only about an inch deep. It's predictive trust rather than vulnerable trust—all surface and no substance. They trust each other to get the job done. Nothing more, nothing less.

Vulnerable trust means telling people hard truths—not out of spite, but because you're looking out for each other's best interests. This constructive accountability helps eliminate fear, improve loyalty, and build high-performing teams.

Now, here's the tricky part: creating vulnerable trust in the workplace can be a bit of a catch-22. You need trust to build high-performing teams, and that trust is built on the kind of deep relationships that are usually built over time. The question, then, is what happens when a new person joins a team? In these situations, we rarely have the luxury to build deep working relationships together. Similarly, it would be antithetical to a culture of love to withhold trust until that new person has "earned" it. If only there were a way to build vulnerable trust quickly *and* effectively.

As it turns out, there is. In 1997, a team of researchers found that they could rapidly create interpersonal relationships between total strangers.[4] Their methodology was fairly straightforward. Starting with a randomly selected group of people, the researchers then split the participants into pairs. In these pairs, the participants took turns asking each other a set of thirty-six questions. Ranging from lighthearted to poignant, these questions included:

> Given the choice of anyone in the world, who would you want as a dinner guest?

> What's your most treasured memory?

> If you could change anything about the way you were raised, what would it be?

Through these questions, the participants began to develop a deep sense of mutual respect and affinity for each other. In fact, many of the participants remained friends long after the experiment—and two even ended up marrying each other.

Essentially, what the researchers found was that vulnerability does not require a preexisting relationship to be effective. Given the right conditions, any two people can connect and begin to build deep, vulnerable trust with each other.

---

4   Arthur Aron, Edward Melinat, Elaine N. Aron, Robert Darrin Vallone, and Renee J. Bator. "The Experimental Generation of Interpersonal Closeness: A Procedure and Some Preliminary Findings." *Personality and Social Psychology Bulletin* 23, no. 4 (April 1997): 363–377. https://doi.org/10.1177%2F0146167297234003

The thirty-six questions exercise successfully creates those conditions, establishing a safe, neutral environment for participants to share their personal experiences with people who, mere moments ago, were complete strangers.[5]

In 2018, driven by our own desire to accelerate the process of building vulnerability-based trust in our organization, we decided to adapt this experiment to a business environment, selecting the most appropriate questions for our purposes and using ourselves as guinea pigs. Even though we knew what to expect, the results were still shocking. Before, we would look around our team and see each other largely in terms of the reports that they owed us, their successes and failures at work, or even how much formal education they had. After, we saw each other as complex, fascinating human beings—people with parents, siblings, partners, and children; people with aspirations and insecurities; people who were just trying to find their way in the world just like everyone else.

Not only did this change how we saw each other, but also how we worked together. If Jeff was working alongside Frank, for instance, and Jeff saw that Frank was having trouble getting something done, Jeff had trust and compassion for Frank's situation. Rather than assume he was lazy or making excuses—or that his lack of a degree meant he was somehow incapable of improving—Jeff saw Frank as a human being who had a problem he was trying to solve.

Encouraged by these results, we then adapted this exercise for our Seneca Leaders workshops to see if we could create

5   Daniel Jones. "The 36 Questions That Lead to Love." *The New York Times*. January 9, 2015.
     https://www.nytimes.com/2015/01/09/style/no-37-big-wedding-or-small.html

an environment of emotional exposure to try and build trust faster among our participants. Once again, the result was breathtaking. Leaders were able to be vulnerable and answer questions that people generally say you shouldn't do at work. The results of these sessions have been incredible. We've seen tears and people hugging during this process. We've heard life-changing stories. People who had worked together side-by-side for a decade or more now saw each other in a completely new light. Participants would walk away with a concentrated dose of trust, and it would transform their ability to work as teams and drive results in their organization.

In July 2019, several months after we had deployed this exercise in our Seneca Leaders program, the University of Sydney released research that validated our approach as more effective than traditional trust-building exercises.[6] Through the thirty-six questions experiment, we've learned how to take a leap of faith and stick the landing. It's not easy to make yourself vulnerable with someone else—whether you've just met or whether you've known that person for years. But if you can, the payoff in trust is almost immediate. When someone sees the faith you're putting in them, even if they might doubt their own abilities, they will not only want to live up to that trust, but also place the same trust in you.

---

6   The University of Sydney. "It Could Pay to Get Personal at Work—Here's Why." July 17, 2019. https://www.sydney.edu.au/news-opinion/news/2019/07/17/It-could-pay-to-get-personal-at-work-heres-why.html

> ### THE SURE SIGNS OF TRUST
>
> How do you know when your teams are practicing vulnerability-based trust? Here are a few sure signs that you have built a high-performing team where each person cares for each other:
>
> - Team members know that their deficiencies won't be used against them.
> - Team members are quick to resolve disputes and conflicts with each other and don't stoop to gossip or slander.
> - Team members begin to act without concern for protecting themselves.
> - Team members have more than a surface-level knowledge of those they work with.

TRUST IN YOUR FULL SELF

Frank still struggles with impostor syndrome when he goes into meetings with clients. No matter how many times he has proven himself, no matter how much he has accomplished, he still goes in feeling as if he has something to prove.

But Jeff, Chris, and Mohammad all know this about Frank. As a result, they go into these same meetings with an eye to offer support and keep him firing on all cylinders. Through this deep, vulnerable trust, Frank is able to relax and be himself.

Here's the thing with impostor syndrome: it never really goes away. But you can ignore it and let it fester, or you can acknowledge it and limit its impact. That's precisely why Frank chose to tell this story here in our fourth Pillar of Love. After all, what better way to confront those pesky impostor feelings than to tell the world one of your deepest insecurities?

In that way, the story in this chapter is just the next iteration of a choice Frank made long ago: to trust his teammates with the knowledge of his full self—and whatever perceived flaws that might entail. Some weren't open to that kind of trust, and they punished him for his vulnerability. After Frank had experienced this enough times, it would have been understandable if he chose to shut down and not share with anyone else.

But it wouldn't have gotten him anywhere. The more we shut down, the more we turn away from trust and vulnerability, the more we feel out of step with those around us, and the more alone we grow. Frank chose the harder path instead— and the long-term benefits of that choice far outweighed any short-term pains.

By sharing who he truly was with his teammates, Frank now has allies who trust and protect him. He has learned he can trust them on a deeper level, and that that trust runs both ways. In that way, Frank has learned that when you trust in your team and you know they have your back, any supposed shortcomings no longer define you. They just become part of your full self.

GET VULNERABLE. GET TRUSTIN'

Find our free vulnerability toolkit and more trust resources at LoveAsA BusinessStrategy.com.

CHAPTER 8

EMPOWERMENT

We hope you got a good dose of empathy for Frank in that last chapter—because now we're going to show you what it looks like when he misbehaves.

In February 2020, right before COVID-19 hit the US in a big way, Softway was preparing for a number of big marketing opportunities/initiatives—conferences, speaking engagements, workshops, you name it. Also around that time, Frank was feeling really, really good about himself—and he had every reason to. After all, he had lost about eighty-five pounds over the past year, and he was—quite literally—a totally different person.

It was a new year, a new round of Softway initiatives, and a new Frank. So, Frank figured it was also time for a new headshot. Triple-chin Frank was no more, and it was time to show off his new look.

As luck would have it, right around that time we were also gearing up for a two-day photo shoot for one of our campaigns. Because the team was going to be taking pictures already, Frank figured there'd be no harm in popping in, snapping off a few photos, and then popping back out. Easy-peasy.

All that was left to do was to let Maggie know his plans.

"Nope," Maggie said flatly when he brought up his big idea.

Well, *that* wasn't the answer Frank expected to hear. "Uh, why?"

"That's not what this shoot is for," she said. "We'll have to do headshots another time."

"But...but my face has changed," Frank said sheepishly. "I don't look like my old picture anymore. It will only take a minute."

Maggie nodded. "You look great. Really. But if I let you get a new headshot, it opens up the floodgates and pushes back our deliverables. I can't do it."

"I understand. That's totally fine," Frank said.

But it wasn't fine. At the time, Maggie was relatively new to Softway, and still a junior project manager. Frank could see why they had hired her and admired her for setting boundaries, but *come on*. A headshot would take five minutes—tops. How could that possibly set back deliverables for the shoot?

Frank decided it was time to do a little misbehavin'.

The next day, Frank walked up to a different project manager.

"Hey, uh, could you ask Maggie if we have time to sneak in a headshot during that photo shoot?"

A few minutes later, the project manager came back. "Maggie said, and I quote, 'Please tell Frank that this photoshoot is not for headshots.' Sorry, Frank."

Dang. Maggie was good.

But Frank was undeterred. He was going to get that new headshot, darn it. The world needed to see his transformation.

Soon, the day of the photoshoot arrived. Frank was dressed to impress. Meanwhile, the photo shoot was going off without a hitch. People were laughing and having a great time as one of our team members snapped shot after marvelous shot.

Soon, it was time for lunch, and the photographer walked over to Frank, who had been patiently (but quite conspicuously) waiting around.

"Hey, Frank," he said, "I've got a few minutes before I head off to lunch. I hear you were hoping to get a new headshot."

Victory!

Frank stood up to accept...and then sat right back down. He couldn't quite explain it, but suddenly he felt gross.

"No thanks, man."

"Are you sure? It's really no trouble," the photographer said.

"I know, but today is not about headshots. It's about marketing deliverables."

The photographer nodded and shrugged it off, then headed off to get some lunch.

EMPOWERMENT ISN'T JUST A WORD

At the very last moment, Frank realized that getting that headshot wasn't his call to make. It was Maggie's. It wasn't that the headshot was a big deal—it really wasn't in the scheme of things—but that he'd be going behind Maggie's back to get it done.

That's not what empowerment looks like in a culture of love. Through countless small moments like these, we have learned that empowerment isn't just a word, but an action. If Maggie was empowered to run the photoshoot, then Frank's job as a leader was to step aside and trust that she would do her job to the best of her ability. This means giving her the latitude and flexibility to make decisions, to take ownership of her tasks and responsibilities, and to perform those tasks as she saw fit. As long as she performs her job within the scope and context of the desired business outcomes, she is free to decide what the best path is to get there.

When you are empowered to do your job, you feel valued, trusted, respected, and included. You feel as if you can bring your full self to work, contribute to a culture of love, and help grow the organization.

On the day of the photoshoot, Maggie had decided that the best path to the marketing outcomes we had defined was to cut out all distractions. Once Frank reminded himself that this was her decision to make, he saw his own behavior in a different light. Maggie was well within her rights to tell Frank "nope," and yet he responded by trying to manipulate the situation to get his way. Had Frank followed through with his plan, he would have effectively told Maggie that her authority wasn't real—which would have broken her trust and significantly hampered her ability to do her job from that point forward. It would also have set a very stark precedent—leaders don't really believe in the culture of love when they don't get their way.

Luckily, at the last minute, Frank's good nature won out. Instead of disempowering Maggie, he owned up to his misbehaviors and apologized to her the next day.

And then, a few weeks later, working through the appropriate channels, Frank got his new headshot. (And he looked *good*.)

CLEAR THE PATH

In a culture of love, empowering a team member isn't about putting someone in charge and then ignoring them. It's about setting them up for success. When choosing to empower one of your teammates with a new responsibility, ask yourself:

- Have you given this person everything they need, including explaining the outcomes and goals you expect?
- Have you given them coaching?
- Are you spending the time to mentor and nurture someone in their role?
- Have you given them information, tools, and the access they need to be successful?
- Are you removing blocks and obstacles?
- Do you respect their decisions, even when those decisions inconvenience you?

When approaching empowerment from a growth mindset, you can remain engaged and available without intervening or micromanaging the process. Instead of handing your team members answers, you clear a path for them so they can arrive at the answers themselves. It can be difficult sometimes to avoid the impulse to intervene, but we've seen time and again that when you give them a chance, people will rise to the occasion.

THE POWER OF EMPOWERMENT

If we had ended the chapter with the story of Frank and Maggie, you probably wouldn't have noticed anything missing. But the truth is, that story is only Empowerment 101. Now it's time for Empowerment 202: Executing in a High-Stakes Situation.

Our Seneca Leaders program began with an impossible task. One day, the program didn't exist at all. The next day, it was the center of a multimillion-dollar business opportunity. To make a long story short, one of our main clients had seen our transformation to a culture of love, and they were impressed—so impressed, in fact, that they wanted us to teach our secret sauce to their leaders. And they were willing to pay us a lot of money to do it.

We were thrilled at the opportunity, not only for the revenue, but also for the chance to teach what we had learned. But there was just one problem: we had never considered making our teachings a product or an experience for our clients. Up until that moment, we had only used these lessons for our own leaders and team members. All of a sudden, we had a brand-new business opportunity—and we only had two weeks to sort out the details.

Suddenly, we were swimming in logistics. How do you design two days' worth of love-based content for twenty-five business leaders? Where could we find a good venue and caterers on such short notice? What did we need to include in the experience that would justify a multimillion-dollar investment?

Full of questions but short on answers, Mohammad bravely dove into the challenge headfirst—and quickly found that he was in way over his head. The more he got done, the more he realized how much he had to do, and the more he realized he didn't know what he was doing. Facing down a growing mountain of challenges, Mohammad let go of the massive workload he'd been holding onto and decided to ask for help. So, he reached out to a power trio of project managers—Erin, Ashley, and Chelsie.

As it turned out, our power trio had deep pockets of knowledge that we had been completely unaware of. Chelsie had an extensive background in event planning, and Erin and Ashley had broad knowledge and logistical experience from working in the service industry. Before we knew it, we had a venue, a caterer, and a working document of how we would run the show (which we still use to this day).

Here is where trust and vulnerability intersect with empowerment. With Erin, Ashley, and Chelsie, we embraced vulnerability-based trust from the get-go. We looked them right in the eye, admitted that we had no idea what we were doing, and asked for help. We had never seen them—or any of our PMs—manage a project like this. But we did know who they were and what they were capable of, so we put our fate in their hands.

They rose above and beyond what we possibly could have expected. For the next two weeks, Erin, Ashley, and Chelsie did everything in their power to make the event a success. No detail was too small. Music cues? Check. Ambient lighting? Check. Greenery and other small decorative touches to create an inviting space? Check. Had we continued to try to manage the process ourselves, all these little details would have been missed—and yet it was precisely these details that made all the difference.

Soon, the big day was upon us, and we were ready to execute. And while we'd love to say that everything went off without a hitch, that was not the case. During the pilot event, mistakes were made.

Here's where the real power of empowerment happens. Because we had given our power trio full ownership of the process, not only were they able to roll with the punches, but they were able to turn a potentially disastrous situation into a big win.

The near-disaster started when we realized that we hadn't

ordered enough food—not by a long shot. As the food began to run out, we watched in horror as attendees began to grumble and get antsy.

Luckily, Ashley was on it. The moment she realized the situation, she got Frank's attention, and together they alerted Mohammad. "These people are struggling," Frank said. "If we don't feed them soon, they're going to leave and go find it themselves. I don't care if we order pizza—we need to do something. "

"Okay," Mohammad said. "Let's get pizza!"

Ashley made the call, hopped in her car, and returned with twenty boxes of fresh, delicious pizza just forty-five minutes later.

Leaders can try as much as they want to prevent their teams from making mistakes. But by doing so, they lose sight of the opportunities for growth that mistakes provide us. Even worse, they deny their team members opportunities to take on new challenges, push the organization in unexpected directions, or, in this case, recognize a problem and work creatively to find a solution on the fly.

We made a mistake not ordering enough food for the workshop. But we also took full ownership of the situation. While Ashley was out getting pizza, Mohammad was apologizing to our attendees for our oversight. He admitted the error, explained that we'd never run this program before, and then explained what we were doing to make it right.

The attendees were blown away (and not just because we

fed them delicious pizza). In fact, as a few of them explained afterward, our little mishap gave them a chance to see our teachings play out in real-time. During a tense situation, we showed them how we loved, cared for, empowered, and trusted each other. This unscripted display not only humanized us, but also made a more compelling case for a culture of love than all our carefully crafted content. At that moment, our attendees saw that we weren't merely consultants looking to win a bid, but practitioners on a mission to change hearts and minds.

Not long after, our client awarded us the contract. Today, the Seneca Leaders program has helped us teach love as a business strategy to thousands of leaders around the world.

PRACTICE IN THE SMALL MOMENTS

Empowerment isn't easy. For many leaders, it goes directly against some of their strongest impulses. That's why it's so important to practice in the small moments, such as when Frank tried to maneuver around Maggie so he could get a new headshot. After all, if you can honor the value of true empowerment when there isn't much on the line, you can do it in the big moments too—when the difference between success or failure could have far-reaching consequences for your business.

In the two weeks leading up to our Seneca Leaders pilot, our commitment to empowerment was frequently put to the test. Mohammad will be the first to admit that relinquishing control wasn't easy for him, and he would often step in and try to be more hands-on in the planning process.

Every time he did, the answer was always the same. "Moham-mad, relax. We've got this. Please *leave us alone* so we can do what we need to do."

This wasn't easy for Mohammad to hear, but eventually, something clicked, and he stepped out of Erin, Ashley, and Chelsie's way for good and let them work their magic. It was at that moment that our team began firing on all cylinders. Even with our project managers' help, prepping a pilot in two weeks was a grind. But for those of us who went through it, it was also one of our favorite experiences working at Softway.

When you empower someone from a place of vulnerability, when that person sees that you trust and believe in them, it unlocks what we call the power of empowerment. From that point on, the person will go out of their way to do whatever they can to excel—not out of fear, but because they want to reward the trust you put in them. This is the feeling that made all those long nights worth it—and what made the Seneca Leaders pilot such a resounding success, mistakes and all.

BRINGING SENECA TO YOU

Since 2018, the Seneca Leaders program has helped thousands of leaders bring a culture of love to their organizations. And we've gotten a lot better at it since that first pilot.

If you are interested in learning more about Seneca Leaders or hosting an event for your organization, please visit LoveAsABusinessStrategy.com.

CHAPTER 9

FORGIVENESS

It was 2017. Softway was now two years into its embrace of love as a business strategy, and Mohammad was proud of what his company had accomplished. Softway had changed rapidly, a process that required both personal and organizational sacrifice. But, at least from Mohammad's perspective, it was working. They had a culture of love. It was fragile, but it was there, and it was a huge accomplishment.

Mohammad held an all-hands meeting in India to talk about the change. He was ready to celebrate what they had all accomplished together after two years of hard work.

To open the meeting, he asked what he thought would be a simple question: "How many of you believe that trust has improved between you and me?"

Two people raised their hands.

Out of a hundred.

Mohammad felt absolutely gutted, like he had been punched

in the stomach. How could no one trust him? Were all those policy changes and the pains he went through to implement them useless? Had the last two years of early mornings and late nights been in vain? Had all the work he'd done to adopt and embody a culture of love meant nothing?

What a disappointment. Mohammad had given up his savings, his car, and his salary to save the company, and now he worried that it had been for nothing. To keep from lashing out and saying something that would make the moment even more embarrassing, Mohammad abruptly ended the meeting and hurried out of the room.

It took Mohammad two days of hard introspection before he knew what he should do.

Despite all the good choices he and the company had made over the past two years, Mohammad had never held himself accountable to the person he was *before* embracing the path of love. That Mohammad had hurt people, leaving a trail of fear, stress, and unforgiveness in his wake. And yet, for all these failings, he had never apologized. He had never said he was in the wrong. Mohammad may have improved his behavior, but his team hadn't forgotten—or forgiven—the person he once was.

It was time to say he was sorry and back it up with action.

Toward the end of his visit, Mohammad held another meeting with the same group. Standing before them, his stomach in knots, he began to speak.

"I realize that I was asking you to trust me when I didn't show you trust first." He paused a moment to gather himself. "I want to apologize for the trouble both my behavior and my policies have caused you. I am sorry to everyone, both to current and former employees and their families. I know that I have caused you harm, and I want to do better."

Then, Mohammad held up the two-year contract that every employee in India had signed. In the contract, his team members had agreed to pay Softway $2,500 if they quit before the two years were up.

"This contract is another sign that I have not demonstrated trust in you." He began tearing the contract in half. "From here on out, none of you are obligated to this contract. If you choose to leave, I understand, and I will not seek damages. Please forgive me."

By that point, Mohammad was in tears. He felt ashamed and alone, humbled in front of people he was supposed to be leading. Once again, overcome by his own emotions, he ended the meeting and left the hall.

Mohammad had recovered and worked hard during the rest of the trip. On the last night, he attended a farewell gathering, where his team presented him with an unexpected surprise: a book filled with messages for him from everyone in the company. The title of that book was *We Love You and We Trust You, Moh.*

It had his name on the title of the book! He broke down. He couldn't stop smiling and crying both—he was so happy. They had heard him. They *trusted* him. They had seen his heart.

A week earlier, his team had greeted Mohammad with skepticism and distrust. Now, they had embraced him as a leader worthy of their trust, support, and love. His authenticity and humility had opened a door that had been tightly shut.

Only two people quit as a result of Mohammad's tearing up that contract. He had been afraid of a mass exodus. But he'd also known he couldn't expect them to trust him unless he trusted them first, and truly owned up to what he had done.

> Forgiveness is the ability to look past someone's mistakes, shortcomings, or offensive actions, and continue to build a relationship.

FORGIVENESS IS A VERB

In Christianity, there's an axiom that God forgives, putting the bad things people have done as far from them as the east is from the west. In Western culture, this idea is often expressed as "forgive and forget."

But let's be honest. We're all human. We may forgive, but we never forget completely. When Mohammad's team in India forgave him in grand fashion, it wasn't as if they all experienced collective amnesia from that moment onward. They still remembered who Mohammad had been for several years, but they chose to love, trust, and pursue a productive relationship with him anyway.

In any relationship—but especially in a business context—this is important to understand. After all, forgiveness is not a one-and-done event, but rather an ongoing process. For the people that we love, whether in a personal or professional context, our empathy and forgiveness require constant renewal. Mohammad may have earned his team's forgiveness during that trip to India, for instance, but that doesn't mean he has never made a mistake or unintentionally harmed them since.

It is through this process of renewal that we can best understand what forgiveness means in a culture of love. Forgiveness is the ability to look past mistakes and continue to build a relationship even if you've been harmed. Bumps and bruises are going to happen along the way. We all unintentionally hurt each other. But if we can all understand that, then we can learn to forgive in a bidirectional way. Teams can forgive leaders. Leaders can forgive teams. And team members can forgive each other.

Of course, for forgiveness to work, team members must be active in the process. Mohammad didn't earn forgiveness when he pivoted the company toward a culture of love. He earned forgiveness when he acknowledged the harm he had caused, committed to repairing it, and stepped up and asked for forgiveness.

AN APOLOGY WITHOUT ACTION...

As an action, this process of asking for forgiveness isn't particularly difficult to understand. However, for most of us, it takes an incredible amount of vulnerability to be willing to take the leap—and making ourselves that vulnerable can be challenging. But with great vulnerability comes great reward. Just look at Mohammad's story: it wasn't until he could make himself vulnerable and ask forgiveness that Softway could fully embrace love as a business strategy and move forward as a company. In a very real way, our entire future as a company hinged on that moment.

Not every leader is capable of doing this. In fact, we know of very few who routinely ask their teams for forgiveness—though it's something nearly all leaders could do more of. To build trust and move forward as a team or as an organization, it's essential to acknowledge the harm and ask forgiveness.

Equally important is accountability. Imagine that Jeff and Frank share an office. While they agree to be responsible for their own work areas and to clean up after themselves, lately Jeff has been ignoring that responsibility. Frank brings this up to Jeff, and Jeff apologizes. "I'm so sorry I've been leaving messes lately, Frank," Jeff says. "I'll be better about it from now on."

A day goes by. Then a week. Then a month. And Jeff is still leaving messes.

Frank was happy to forgive Jeff once. But now that he sees Jeff has no real intention to change, he's rightfully upset. Jeff has invalidated his apology and damaged the trust that existed between the two officemates. Where once Jeff had an opportunity to strengthen his relationship with Frank, he has instead harmed it further.

While this particular lesson is hypothetical, the dynamic it illustrates is very real. In situations like this, actions really do speak louder than intentions. Forgiveness loses its potency quickly if no action follows the apology.

This is why self-awareness and communication are such essential pieces in asking for forgiveness. You cannot ask forgiveness if you do not acknowledge fault, which means you must possess the emotional intelligence and self-awareness to know when you have broken someone's trust. Without understanding how you caused this break, you cannot attempt to repair it. Then, to seek true forgiveness, you must communicate your understanding both in speech and action—and in a way that seeks to build relationships rather than tear them down.

YES, FORGIVENESS IS BLIND

As hard as it can be to ask for forgiveness, offering forgiveness can often be even harder. When you feel you've been wronged or hurt, it can be difficult to let go of that feeling. It took two full years *after* Mohammad embraced love as a business strategy before his team in India could forgive him for the hurt he had caused before. Even after Mohammad realized the extent of the harm his actions had caused and offered an apology, it took a leap of faith on the part of his team to look past that hurt and be willing to forgive.

This is the power of the apology. In order to forgive, we must be able to see the goodness in the person we are forgiving. A sincere apology helps bring those qualities front and center, whereas we otherwise might only see the flaws and weaknesses of the person.

That said, we don't always have the benefit of a dramatic apology to consider whether a person deserves forgiveness. In fact, often we receive no apologies at all for the harm we perceive others to have caused—and they might not even be aware they have caused it!

In situations such as these, practicing forgiveness can be especially tricky. It's hard to forget when we've been wronged.

It's hard to let those feelings of unforgiveness go. But it's crucial that we do so. If we don't, we risk harming the very people who have harmed us.

As we said in Chapter 3, unforgiveness is the root of all misbehavior. Unforgiveness compels us to lash out at our teammates, to verbally attack or emotionally abuse them, to play mind games and punish them, to become apathetic or disassociate from our jobs. Unfortunately, no form of misbehavior or act of revenge can release you from the hurt you are feeling. Sure, you might feel some temporary satisfaction by yelling at someone or playing mind games, but that satisfaction is fleeting—and when it's gone, you're right back where you started—or even worse off.

Viewed in this light, forgiveness isn't something we do for others, but something we do for ourselves. It's a way to release ourselves from our pain, to overcome the grudges we hold, and to find peace both within ourselves and with those around us. One of the best approaches we've found to initiate forgiveness is through service. When you are able to serve the very person who has caused you harm, you learn to empathize and connect with that person—through empathy and connection, you will find it in your heart to forgive them.

To be clear, this forgiveness may never be reciprocated. Just as a teammate may never know they have harmed you in the first place, they might never recognize the work you put in to forgive them and move past that harm. At first glance, this might sound like a hard pill to swallow, but in reality, it also doesn't matter. Even if the act of forgiveness is only for you and no one else, it's still worth the effort.

LESS TIME FOR FIGHTING, MORE TIME FOR INNOVATION

Forgiveness improves trust and bolsters psychological safety. It also enables individuals to let go of their prison of unforgiveness and move forward with considerably less emotional baggage. In so doing, it contributes toward more agile, risk-tolerant teams. The greatest byproduct of forgiveness, then, is momentum.

This was why it was so important for Mohammad to ask his team in India for forgiveness. For nearly two years, Mohammad had done everything in his power to move the organization forward—and in many respects, he had succeeded. But the momentum he was looking for still wasn't there. Finally, when he made himself vulnerable and admitted his mistakes, Softway was truly able to move forward.

It doesn't matter what initiative you try to implement or what new process you introduce to your teams to get your company moving. Until you've identified and addressed the elephant in the room and asked for forgiveness—and until you've learned to forgive others without any expectation of reciprocity—all those efforts likely won't amount to much. Unforgiveness will still be simmering underneath everything that happens, eating away at your productivity, trust, and relationships.

A culture that actively practices forgiveness, on the other hand, sees tremendous benefits in productivity, creativity, and innovation. Why? Because when you're not afraid of judgment or punishment, you feel empowered to take risks and think about your work in new and novel ways.

This in turn leads to a more agile organization. When you lose fear, you gain enthusiasm and resilience. Team members will leap at the opportunity to learn from others, address the root causes of a problem, and pivot quickly and effectively. Does everything work out perfectly 100 percent of the time? Absolutely not. However, a culture of love views failure as an opportunity, not as an embarrassing disaster that is just as quickly swept under the rug. In such an environment, we learn not only to forgive others for their perceived errors, but ourselves as well.

Part 3

PUT LOVE
TO WORK

In Part 1, we built the foundation; in Part 2 we set up the Pillars; and here in Part 3, we're going to put a roof over your head.

This part of the book is for the "tangible takeaways" crowd. If you're part of that crowd, thanks for being patient. We know this kind of action-oriented content is your bread and butter, but for anything in this section to make sense, we had to lay some groundwork first.

In the following chapters, we are going to share our growth and transformation as an organization once we embraced a culture of love (including all those sweet, sweet data points and insights you've been craving). We're also going to put love to the test. Can "love" be woven into processes, tools, and hiring practices—the very DNA that makes a business functional? Is love really a *viable option* that can bridge the gap between better cultures and more revenue?

The answer—backed up with data—is yes. And we're about to show you how it's possible.

One last thing before we start. It takes time to see the results you're looking for. But, just like going to the gym, gains are built and sustained over time. When you're in the middle of it, grinding it out every day, you may not even notice that you're making progress and packing muscle. Then, one day, you look in the mirror and realize that a whole new person is standing before you.

The point is, change is often felt before it's measured—but once it's measured, there won't be any room for doubt. Love can be your business strategy too.

CHAPTER 10

TO LEAD IS TO SERVE

It was around 2013, roughly ten years after Mohammad had founded Softway. To that point, Softway had been successful, but he was getting antsy. He wanted more. It was time for Softway to start attracting higher-profile clients and break into the big leagues.

So, he set a new goal: grow the company past $50 million in revenue.

There was just one small problem. Mohammad had never grown a $50 million company. Looking for help to guide the process, he sought out a new executive leadership team—industry vets who had helped oversee explosive growth at companies like IBM and Microsoft.

From the moment they walked into the office, the new leadership brought an old-school sensibility along with them. They looked and acted the part of industry vets. Moreover, they had a plan—the same plan they had used for decades—and they expected everyone to follow it to the letter.

First things first. If he was going to lead a $50 million organization, the executive leadership team argued, then Mohammad had to look and act the part. So, they gave him a set of rules to follow that they felt would change his image for the better:

Separate yourself from your employees. Don't hang out with them on the floor level. Let them know you are the boss and demand respect.

Dress and spend like a CEO. Wear expensive suits, drive a fancy car, and spend lavishly as if money is not an issue. If that means buying a $150,000 Porsche on the company dime, then so be it.

Have a large, executive office that's separated from the rest of the company. Preferably, this should be off in an executive wing and not a place employees will feel comfortable walking through. Oh, and make sure it's the biggest office within the organization.

Never go to anyone with questions. Make them come to you.

These rules had little to do with running a company. They were all about the perception of leadership, about playing the part of "CEO," rather than *being* a CEO. None of it felt right to Mohammad—it all felt artificial.

But what did Mohammad know? For ten years, he'd been going by his gut. Each member of the new executive leadership team had impeccable resumes—and they had brought along plenty of fancy data, pie charts, and graphs to back up each and every rule. Even if Mohammad wanted to speak up, he felt he had little wiggle room to do so.

And so, Scrappy Startup Mohammad slowly transformed into CEO Mohammad—along with all the mindsets and mis-behaviors that came with it. No one particularly liked CEO Mohammad. CEO Mohammad ignored his team members as he walked through the office. CEO Mohammad wrote angry emails about refrigerator etiquette. CEO Mohammad expected that everyone follow his ad hoc meeting schedule, no matter what their own calendars might have said.

CEO Mohammad almost ran his company into the ground. Eventually, Human Being Mohammad had to step in and turn things around.

For roughly three years, Mohammad had tried to play the part of a big-time CEO. But the more he did, the more dis-tance Mohammad created between himself and his team. It wasn't until 2016, when Mohammad embraced love as a business strategy and got back to being himself, that Softway began to turn around.

That's when Human Being Mohammad won out. Instead of trying to impress people, Mohammad spent his time imple-menting his vision for what a culture of love could look like at his company. A more authentic Mohammad meant a more authentic—and ultimately higher-performing—Softway.

Granted, this didn't come without its challenges. While CEO Mohammad ultimately proved to be a bad fit, the choice did make some sense—that is, many business leaders really *do* expect CEOs to look and act a certain way. After Mohammad chose to break that mold, not everyone responded positively.

For instance, one time Mohammad and another Softway

team member were at a meeting with a prospective client. Mohammad arrived at the meeting dressed casually—no fancy suit or expensive watch, just some comfortable slacks and a nice sweater. After the meeting, Mohammad thanked everyone for their time and left the other team member to hammer out the specifics of the project.

As we learned later from our point of contact in the room, the second Mohammad left, one of the VPs at the company spoke up. "I'm sorry, but is this really who we want to work with?" the VP said to his team. "Look at the way this guy dresses. Look at how he talks. He doesn't exactly scream *leadership material.*"

Despite the VP's reservations, the company ultimately awarded Softway the contract—which we delivered on to the letter. Not long after we had fulfilled the contract, that same VP reached out to Mohammad and invited him to lunch.

At lunch, the VP came clean. "Listen, Mohammad, I had this perception of you that was all wrong. I didn't think you carried yourself with the gravitas of a CEO, and we almost didn't give you our business because of it. Now I see what kind of leader you really are, and I just wanted to say that I'm glad I got to work with you. Thank you."

In that VP's transformation, Mohammad saw a reflection of his own. It's easy to become too preoccupied with how leaders carry themselves, how their office looks, or what kinds of cars they drive. That version of leadership will not work anymore. In a culture of love, leaders aren't focused on the trappings of their role, but rather on how they *conduct* themselves—on which behaviors they bring to work, how they interact with others, and how they lead and inspire their teams.

In this chapter, we're going to share the story of Mohammad's transformational journey from traditional leadership to servant leadership. Before we do, we want to reiterate an important point. Leadership isn't just for the members of the C-Suite. You don't have to be the CEO of your company to adopt the principles of servant leadership found in this chapter. No matter where your position on the org chart, you can be a leader within your role. While we use Mohammad's story to illustrate what servant leadership might look like, his is only one possible path. Your journey is your own.

So, as we move through this story, we encourage you to take the lessons Mohammad learned, do some introspection, and apply instances of servant leadership that make sense to you in your leadership journey. If there's one thing we hope you take away from this story, it's this: get rid of the things that are preventing you from serving people better. If it's a physical possession, then start working against it. If it's too many meetings on your calendar that are preventing you from mentoring and serving those around you, find a way to reduce the load. However you can, find the area of your life that is taking your focus away, and address it.

"WHAT THE HECK IS SERVANT LEADERSHIP?"

In 2015, only two weeks after Mohammad witnessed the University of Houston's miraculous comeback and began steering Softway toward a culture of love, a few of us had the opportunity to visit the Southwest Airlines headquarters in Dallas Love Field. We were looking forward to the visit for a few reasons. First, Southwest was interested in working with us, and we were excited about the business opportunity. Second, a licensed pilot himself, Mohammad was thrilled to see all the planes on display at Southwest's corporate headquarters.

But as he walked the storied halls of Southwest Airlines, it wasn't the planes that caught his eye, but rather a big, attention-grabbing sign that simply read: SERVANT LEADERSHIP.

Wait, what the heck is servant leadership? Mohammad thought to himself.

Mohammad had never come across this term before—and at first glance, he wasn't sure he understood its meaning. The words *servant* and *leader* together? It just didn't seem right.

To Mohammad, his understanding of *servant* was greatly influenced by Indian society, which has traditionally followed a tiered system. At the bottom, there are servants. At the top, there are leaders. And servants usually served the leaders. To Mohammad, then, the very idea of a servant leader was a contradiction. How could someone possibly be both at the same time?

As confused as he was, Mohammad was also deeply curious. Clearly, there was something he was missing. So, he began doing some research. As he discovered, servant leadership is a philosophy and set of practices in which leaders put the needs of the team before themselves—thereby creating an environment where the team can be successful in an entirely new way. As the Greenleaf Center for Servant Leadership says, "Servant leadership enriches the lives of individuals, builds better organizations, and ultimately creates a more just and caring world."

The more Mohammad learned, the more he understood why Southwest Airlines had gone to such lengths to display that banner so prominently at their headquarters. In many ways, Southwest is the embodiment of the servant leadership philosophy—and it is this point of difference that makes their service and customer experience so good compared to those of other airlines. They paint hearts on their planes, their employees actually smile, and they stick to their philosophy of not trying to deceive people with nickel-and-dime charges on top of fares. They also take customer dissatisfaction seriously and act quickly to resolve any problems.

Servant leadership isn't just a fad at Southwest Airlines. It's what led them to become profitable for forty-six straight years leading into the COVID-19 pandemic, and even *that* hasn't stopped them from innovating (see Chapter 14). Southwest's co-founder and former CEO, Herb Kelleher, actively practiced servant leadership—hanging out with his team, spearheading culture initiatives, and even jumping in to help lighten the load of the baggage crew.

The more Mohammad learned, the more he was inspired. And this discovery couldn't have come at a better moment. Servant leadership was a natural fit for the culture of love he was trying to build at Softway, and Southwest offered the perfect example of this practice in action.

From that moment on, Mohammad was all-in. No more putting himself first as a leader. No more obsessing over appearances. His number-one duty was to serve others, to create a safe environment for his team, and to remove any barriers to their success. And that was exactly what he was going to do.

> A culture of love is enabled and embodied through servant leadership. This practice is not just a "nice thing to have." It is essential.

THE 10 PRINCIPLES OF SERVANT LEADERSHIP

Like so many things in life, servant leadership doesn't come with an on/off switch. Mohammad didn't just learn about servant leadership one day after a visit to Southwest, decide to do it, and then never think about it again. As Mohammad would be the first to tell you, servant leadership is a journey with no destination—and one that he is still on today. However, in 2016, before he could even get started, first he had to mend all the bridges that CEO Mohammad had burned.

This was no small task. Mohammad's chronic misbehaviors (many of which we have shared in this book) had created a lot of mistrust and unforgiveness, and it took him years to regain his organization's trust. At times, Mohammad worried that the damage he had caused might be irreversible, but he was determined to try anyway.

As we said, the journey isn't over, and Mohammad and the rest of us still have a lot to learn about servant leadership ourselves. But we've also learned a lot along the way. The following 10 Principles of Servant Leadership are time-tested and battle-worn. While the journey of servant leadership might be long and uncertain, these principles will help you start off on the right foot.

PRINCIPLE #1: PUT OTHERS' NEEDS FIRST

Initially, the needs of leadership—especially the needs of CEO Mohammad—came before anyone else's. Softway team members knew this all too well, which is why they dismissed Mohammad's new focus on servant leadership as nothing more than a bunch of hot air. We tried as hard as we could to explain the value of this new approach—and that our own needs would take a back seat to theirs—but our words went in one ear and out the other.

But as the old cliché goes, actions speak louder than words. It was one thing to *say* that we wanted to put team members' needs before our own, but it was another thing to do it. The problem was, we didn't know what our team members' needs were. They were so jaded after so many years of abuse that they wouldn't open up to us.

Here is where our empathy pillar becomes so important: our lives are rich and nuanced. Whatever someone thinks you are like on the surface, there's always a lot more going on behind the scenes. This is the case for everyone, regardless of where you might fit within your organization. The lesson for leaders—the one that we took—is that we should never assume we know what people are dealing with.

Instead, you have to put in the work and find out. Ask questions. Engage with them. Learn about your team members. If you suspect there's a problem lurking under the surface, don't ignore it—dive in and uncover it.

If Mohammad was going to get his team members to open up to him, he had to prove his own intentions were sincere. So, he moved out of his big, fancy CEO office and moved into the bullpen so he could work side-by-side with his team and better support their needs. No more awkward walks through the executive suite. If his team members needed something, he would be right there to help them. Being in the bullpen also made Mohammad more visible—and Mohammad wanted his team to see that he was there all the time. For the next year, he was the first person to show up to the office and the last person to leave. If other team members were staying late, he would order them dinner. Whatever it took to be present and supportive, he would do it. Through every action, Mohammad embodied the principle of putting others' needs before his own.

PRINCIPLE #2: BE HUMBLE AND PRACTICE GRATITUDE

Be humble enough to learn, and vulnerable enough to apologize. During the CEO Mohammad years, Mohammad never once wrote a thank-you note. Not one.

Human Being Mohammad went all-in on gratitude, sending out personalized, handwritten notes to everyone in the office. For instance, if a team member was quietly putting in long hours, Mohammad wrote them a note so they would know their effort wasn't going unnoticed. Often, these notes would come with gift cards as well—a subtle nudge to the team member to take a night off every once in a while and take their family to dinner.

Not only did Mohammad want his team members to feel noticed, but he also wanted them to know he wasn't above them. For years, every time he traveled to our India office, he only made time to meet with the leadership there. He saw no reason to speak with anyone else.

When Mohammad embraced servant leadership, however, that changed. Now when he traveled to India, he spoke with everyone—including the janitorial staff. He made it a point to take team members out to lunch or dinner, and to learn about their lives, their families, and their ambitions. With over a hundred team members in India, this meant a lot of meals over the course of a five-day trip. So, while he always came back to Houston a little heavier, he also came back a lot more fulfilled.

He also often came back with gifts for his Houston team. On one trip, for instance, he brought back Indian bangles and anklets for the women in the office and Indian shirts (or *kurtas*) for the men. But he didn't stop there; Mohammad also brought back gifts for team members' kids as well.

So why did Mohammad go to all this trouble—and how was he able to fit so many gifts into his luggage? Because he wanted to show gratitude for his team members, to demonstrate through action that he was thinking about them and that he cared about their well-being. In his journey to becoming a servant leader, his team had given him the gift of feedback (even if that feedback didn't always paint him in the best light). To show his appreciation and to demonstrate humility for what his team had done for them, bringing along a few gifts was the least he could do.

As for the luggage question, that remains a mystery. A leader has to keep some secrets, after all.

PRINCIPLE #3: DO NOT ASK OTHERS TO DO SOMETHING THAT YOU ARE NOT WILLING TO DO

Before a servant leader asks someone to do something, they're prepared to do it themselves. They know all contributions are worthwhile, no matter how small or menial. Mohammad learned this when he made it a point to learn and perform other roles in the company, and Chris learned this as well when Sunil confronted him with the untenable workload problem in HR (see Chapter 8).

For Mohammad, learning all the different roles was his way of demonstrating that he was willing to do whatever was needed to help his employees—serving them food, cleaning the office, giving them rides, whatever it took. To a servant leader, no task is beneath you. If you expect your employees to clean up after each other or make a new pot of coffee, then you must also be willing to do those things yourself. Small actions speak volumes. If you're careful to sweat the little things, then your team will be too—and your organization will be better for the effort.

This boots-on-the-ground approach also taught Mohammad a thing or two about his own policies. For instance, when he took on the role of project manager, he struggled. The processes put in place for a project manager were simply too much to keep up with. But Mohammad couldn't complain— after all, *he* was the one who put those processes in place. If he couldn't do the job himself, then he had no business asking his PMs to do it, either!

PRINCIPLE #4: ASSUME GOOD INTENT

Prior to 2016, Softway had installed biometric scanners in our offices. We told team members that the scanners enhanced security (and that was true), but we also used them to track their movements. We knew exactly when they arrived at work, and exactly when they left. If they showed up late or left early, we docked their pay (for the full story, see Chapter 13).

After we shifted to a culture of love, we dismantled this system as part of our campaign to re-establish trust among our teams. Today, it only exists as a piece of our history—a bold reminder of how *not* to treat those who are working to propel your company forward.

That said, the problem wasn't with the tools themselves. It was with our motivation for using them. If you couldn't tell by now, CEO Mohammad had anger management issues. A lot of these issues were fueled by how he viewed Softway's employees. He assumed bad intent in nearly everyone—that they were constantly trying to get one over on us and get paid for doing nothing. The biometric system was an emblem of that distrust, and its influence could be felt throughout the organization. Eventually, just about everyone had adopted the same pessimistic outlook as Mohammad.

In business theory, an authoritarian company that assumes the bad intent of all its employees is known as a *Theory X* organization. For instance, if there is a policy being abused, the organization will remove or amend that policy. Today, Softway takes a *Theory Y* approach—that is, we are a participative organization that assumes that all our team members operate with good intent. If a policy is being abused, we address the issue with the offenders rather than punish the entire organization.

This wasn't an easy transition. Not only did the legacy of our misbehaviors cast a long shadow, but it was sometimes difficult to break old habits. In fact, it required us to go against our very nature. As humans, when we see someone make a choice that we disagree with, our first impulse is to assume that person is acting in bad faith. In fact, usually the opposite is true. People generally operate in good faith.

Assuming good intent, in other words, takes active practice—which is precisely what makes it such an important part of servant leadership. It doesn't matter whether you're in a conversation in the hallway, participating in a meeting, or learning about a choice someone made that didn't work out. When you assume good intent, you approach that moment with genuine trust and empathy. As a result, you're far more willing to see the situation from the other person's perspective (and nullify all those misbehaviors we outlined in Chapter 3). It's hard to turn inward and feel persecuted when you're focused on your team member's perspective rather than your own.

PRINCIPLE #5: LOOK FOR THE GOOD IN OTHERS AND FIND THE WEAKNESSES IN YOURSELF

This principle works in lockstep with Principle #4. Not only should you assume good intent, but you should also focus on the positives in others instead of dwelling on any of the negatives. Once again, this is easier said than done.

Mohammad knew that, in order to embody a culture of love, he as a CEO would have to learn to love his team. This didn't come naturally for him—how can you love your team when you're so accustomed to zeroing in on all their mistakes and bad behaviors? Finally, one of Mohammad's mentors helped him see the error of his ways. In order to love his team, Mohammad must look for their good qualities rather than look for the bad.

In our personal lives, this is easy for most of us to do. In a loving relationship, we're more than willing to look past the bad and focus on the good these relationships represent.

Despite what we may believe, there's no reason our working relationships can't operate in the same way.

As a servant leader, your job is to serve your team as a positive role model and to bring out the best in them. If they make a mistake or if their bad qualities begin to shine through, a servant leader must be willing to look past these flaws and weaknesses to see all the good qualities too.

Here's the catch: while servant leaders must be willing to look past the mistakes and misbehaviors of their teams, they must constantly be on the lookout for their own. After all, we all have weaknesses, regardless of our status inside the organization. Through constant introspection and self-awareness, you can identify your flaws and work to become a better leader.

But whatever you uncover, don't be too hard on yourself. Sure, you might misbehave or make mistakes from time to time, but don't forget all the good you're capable of too. In other words, we're always under construction—learning from our mistakes and working on getting better.

PRINCIPLE #6: RESPOND INSTEAD OF REACT

Imagine you're in a crowded restaurant with your family. All of a sudden, a cockroach appears on the table, and you and the rest of your family begin to scream. As you leap from the table, you frantically start swatting at the cockroach, but it flies off and lands on another table—sending that group into a frenzy too. The cockroach escapes again, this time landing on yet another unsuspecting diner's back.

Then, before the diner realizes what's going on, a waiter calmly walks over, grabs the cockroach, and tosses it outside.

Feeling squeamish yet?

Don't worry, this is all hypothetical. No diners (or cockroaches) were harmed in the telling of this story.

Here's the moral of the story: while the customers at the first two tables *reacted*, the waiter *responded*—and that distinction made all the difference.

When we only react to situations—that is, when we leap before we look—chaos usually follows. And where there's chaos, there's misbehavior. We blow up, we exaggerate the issue, and we fail to assume good intent. Servant leaders, on the other hand, *respond*. They are calm in the face of challenges. They do their best to consider all parties involved, and then choose the best course of action available to them. And when they don't (because they're human and make mistakes) they own up to it.

PRINCIPLE #7: KNOW THAT POWER DOES NOT EQUAL LEADERSHIP

If you've never had the privilege of flying from Houston to Bengaluru, you're missing out—on about twenty-seven hours of travel for a one-stop flight (if you're lucky). To put it mildly, it's a little bit of an ordeal, one that Mohammad and other members of the Houston team make about four times a year.

For years, however, while Mohammad would fly business class, the rest of the Softway team was relegated to economy class. It was easy to justify this disparity from a business perspective. Mohammad flew more, the company couldn't afford to upgrade everyone to business class, and also, Mohammad was the CEO. Sure, he felt guilty about it, but until 2016, he wasn't prepared to do anything about it.

As he pivoted to servant leadership, however, Mohammad did a lot of introspection, and he realized that's not how a servant leader would act. So, he began flying economy with the rest of the Houston crew. To his surprise, it wasn't that bad. He loved the opportunity to connect with the rest of his team and strengthen those relationships. From that perspective, the move to economy class wasn't a sacrifice at all—it was an upgrade!

This isn't to say there weren't challenges. Everyone enjoyed seeing more of Mohammad on the flight, but not everyone enjoyed sitting next to him. As Chris will be the first to tell you, Mohammad has what he affectionately calls "sleep tremors." There's nothing scary or dangerous about them. But if you're sitting next to Mohammad while he sleeps, you're going to end up with some bruised ribs thanks to all the constant twitching and jabbing—not to mention that you're not going to get a wink of sleep yourself.

While the social aspect of Mohammad's move to economy class was a resounding success, the sleep and comfort aspect was still sorely lacking. Team members were arriving in Houston or Bengaluru jet-lagged and exhausted—and their jam-packed schedules offered them little chance to catch up on any sleep. So, as soon as Softway could afford the additional cost, Mohammad made sure everyone got to fly business class. It may be a larger expense (business class tickets generally run five times higher than economy class), but it was the right thing to do.

PRINCIPLE #8: TAKE CARE OF OTHERS (WHO IN TURN WILL TAKE CARE OF YOU)

In the most desperate days of Softway's downturn, we were staring at over seven figures in debt, our credit line had been maxed out, and we were behind on rent for our office. When Mohammad asked, "Will we be able to open our doors tomorrow?" it wasn't hyperbole.

As bleak as things looked, Mohammad wasn't going to give up on his team. As long as they were fighting to keep the company in business, he was going to fight to keep them employed. This meant pulling out all the stops:

> He mortgaged his fully paid-off home and put the money into the business to make payroll.

> He sold his Porsche (a relic of his CEO Mohammad days) and put the money back into the company. His new ride became Softway's 2011 Toyota Sienna minivan (which he still drives today).

> He stopped taking a paycheck for eight months so his employees could get paid.

None of these decisions were easy, but it felt good helping others. And his sacrifices didn't go unnoticed. By putting others' needs before his own, Mohammad inspired the rest of his team to go all-in for the company as well. Executives in both our American and Indian offices took pay cuts to help out—including Jeff, who declined all pay for two months. Some team members—for example, our financial controller, Taban—declined a salary entirely until Mohammad started taking one for himself again. (Taban also conspired with Jeff to keep the latter's refusal of salary a secret.) Elsewhere in sales, team members gave up commissions and bonuses to make sure the company could stay open.

As Mohammad's spirit of sacrifice trickled through the company, the culture began to transform. Despite the hard times, morale was high. Buoyed by this spirit, Softway began to turn things around.

PRINCIPLE #9: INCLUSION AND BELONGING BEGIN WITH SERVANT LEADERSHIP

Up to this point, Principles 1 through 8 have all been leading to the same place: inclusion. If you are committed to creating an environment of inclusion within your organization, then servant leadership is the first step on the path. Without putting the needs of others before yourself, without practicing gratitude, without assuming good intent in others, there is no inclusion. Period.

This is where you can see the big switch in action between traditional leadership and servant leadership. Traditional leadership states that everything should revolve around the leader, which is a fundamentally passive approach. Servant leadership requires active participation—to speak with your team, hear what they have to say, invite their input, and consider their ideas. Enabling someone to feel heard is one of the best ways to help them grow. The more each individual team member is able to grow, the more your organization will grow along with them. Servant leaders create space and access to make this happen.

PRINCIPLE #10: CHANGE STARTS WITH YOU

For over a decade, Mohammad operated with the mindset that others should be working *for* him, not *with* him. This mindset nearly sank Softway. Fortunately, just before it was too late, Mohammad had an epiphany in the form of an epic University of Houston football victory that changed the company—and our team—for the better.

But this change had to start with Mohammad. As the CEO, he was the one creating the playbook for the company. Although it took him longer than he wished it would have to figure out the best path, he eventually did—and once he did, it was full speed ahead.

You don't need to be a CEO to practice this or any other principle of servant leadership. Anyone can embody the change they want to see in their organization. If you're in a toxic environment at your company, break the cycle and commit to change. Assume the good intentions of those around you and ask yourself how you can better serve those around you. The change won't happen overnight, but the good thing about servant leadership is that it's contagious. The more we work to improve the lives of those around us, the more likely they are to want to do the same.

Just remember, this kind of change isn't passive, and it doesn't happen by chance. Servant leadership is an active choice—one that you must be willing to make every day.

BEING OKAY WITH TOUGH TIMES

Softway has certainly come a long way from the days of CEO Mohammad. For years, he followed the advice of an executive leadership team that was well-intentioned, but that was using an outdated playbook written during a different era of business—an era when the concept of servant leadership wasn't even a blip on their radar.

We have learned firsthand that businesses cannot continue to operate in the same outmoded mindset as we did. After all, it's a competitive world out there, and every organization is looking for an advantage that will put them ahead of their competition. No matter your role in the organization, whether you're a senior executive, a middle manager, or an aspiring leader, if you want to create high-performing teams, you must *serve* those teams by making each person feel like a valued, important part of a well-oiled machine.

That said, a warning. While servant leadership is essential to creating a culture of love, the path can be a lonely one. Servant leadership means supporting those you lead—often without being seen. As such, it can be a quiet and thankless task. There will be tough days, days when no one notices your work or thanks you for what you're doing behind the scenes to help them succeed. You will rarely have opportunities to be publicly recognized for your efforts—and you will have *zero* opportunities to brag about those efforts. That's the nature of the work, and you must be okay with it.

Of course, perhaps even more challenging than the days that no one notices your work are the days that *everyone* notices— the days when you make a big, obvious mistake. Leaders are only human. We screw up just like everyone else. However, every single move, every single behavior, every single action we take (or don't take) will be critiqued, judged, and evaluated at a higher standard than others. Even if you make only one mistake in a sea of otherwise perfect behavior, you will still be judged for that one mistake. And you must be okay with it.

In those moments, no matter how much good you've done or how much goodwill you might have built up, the results can be detrimental. They can send your company back a mile, and you may have to retrace your steps. Regardless of your intention, you'll have to turn around, pick up the pieces, and start over. These are the moments in which others form their perceptions of you, and these perceptions will become a reality in their mind. You must be okay with that too.

As a servant leader, you will be expected to have empathy toward your team members and always do the best for your team, even if your team may not always do the same for you. You will be expected to understand the personal needs of your team members and what they may be experiencing in their personal lives, even if your team may not do the same for you. Finally, you will be expected to trust your team absolutely, even if they do not always show the same trust in you. In all those situations, you must be okay with it.

There will be a lot of work involved. And from your point of view, the balance of work may not always be fair. But there is no fairness in leadership—you must continue to keep moving forward. This will be a lot of responsibility to shoulder, but know this: the sacrifices, the tough times, and the difficulties you go through as a leader *will* show results—and eventually, your efforts *will* be noticed.

How do we know? Because every organization is a reflection of the leaders that build it, piece by piece, day after day. The road may be rocky—not all interactions with your team or your fellow leaders will be smooth, and no interaction is neutral. As a leader, your behaviors have an outsized impact on your culture. Every choice you make is an opportunity to build that culture up or tear it down. *You* set the tone—and for better or worse, others will follow.

In that regard, every time someone celebrates your culture, every time someone celebrates a big organizational win, every time someone shares how happy they are to be doing work that matters, they're celebrating *you* as well.

But to get there, remember this: you cannot expect your culture or anyone around you to develop faster than you do as a leader. You must go first and set the tone for others to follow. If you can do that, then you can become a principal driver of a culture of love.

CHAPTER 11

WE ARE BETTER TOGETHER

Your palms are sweaty, knees weak, arms are heavy (something about mom's spaghetti). Your heart is beating a hundred miles an hour. Your face is flushed, and you can barely breathe.

There is a bomb in front of you. It is counting down...four minutes and ten seconds until it blows up the building. All around you, people are scrambling to evacuate, but you know that unless you act quickly to defuse it, at least two dozen people will be killed or injured in the blast.

There's just one problem: you don't know the first thing about bombs.

Luckily, the team of experts speaking to you over the intercom has the information necessary to defuse it. As long as you can work together as a group to relay the right information back and forth, you and everyone else may just get out of here alive.

Do you feel like you're in a James Bond film yet?

Spoiler alert: there's no real bomb. It's all just a simulation.

We've led this actual "bomb game" exercise with thousands of business leaders over the years—many of whom are established vets with twenty or thirty years of experience in their organizations. When it comes to individual performance, these leaders are generally regarded as the cream of the crop. However, when we asked them to come together as a group, most of them were unable to work together and defuse the digital bomb. Together they are responsible for the loss of hundreds and hundreds of (very imaginary) lives.

Of course, this failure is precisely why we utilize the game in the first place—to illustrate how potentially high-performing teams could operate—and to contrast that with how they often do. Nothing about this challenge is especially difficult; advanced expertise is absolutely not required. The bomb manual is written in simple words in black and white. All the "experts" have to do to win is communicate those instructions to the teammate in charge of defusing the bomb on a computer across the room. The person defusing the digital bomb can't see the instructions, and the "experts" with those precious instructions are hidden behind a partition and can't see the bomb. Sure, there is a time limit and several steps to complete—and everyone in the audience is watching and following along—but if you just keep your cool and communicate, you should be able to get through it.

Some leaders do. After running this exercise enough times, we've learned that the leaders on these successful teams all share a few common elements:

They feel free to speak up.

They will admit ignorance and describe what they do or do not know quickly.

There was no single leader in the group. Team members took turns leading and sharing what they had learned.

Contrast that with the teams that blew up the bomb, ran out of time, or both. We've learned that the members of losing teams often share some common traits as well. Usually, they start by sitting heads-down, staring at the manual. They hardly speak to each other, often because they're either scared or worried they might disrupt what's going on around them. Most importantly, there'd be no trust between the person defusing the bomb and the teammates reading the manual. The person controlling the bomb would describe what they saw to the expert, but wouldn't trust what they heard in return.

"So you want me to cut this wire, right?"

"The fourth wire."

"The fourth from the top counting down?"

"Uhhhh—yes."

"It's a yellow wire. Is that okay?"

"I...think so. Do it."

They'd cut the wire, and it would be right, but the over-communication from lack of trust would eat up so much time that the team would lose.

Now, to be fair, it's okay to be a little cautious when defusing a bomb. This is an (imaginary) life-or-death situation, after all. But here's the thing: it's okay to make some mistakes. If you cut the wrong wire, you don't automatically lose the game—you get three chances! The teams that failed would ignore this fact, paralyzed by not wanting to make even one mistake.

The successful teams, on the other hand, trusted each other— even enough to make mistakes.

"Cut the fourth wire."

"Oh. That was wrong."

"Okay, what happened?"

"I see what I did. I think it's the yellow one. Should I try that one instead?"

"Actually, yes, I think the yellow one is right."

"Okay. It's cut."

"Great! Now I need you to find the green button."

The successful team may have made a mistake, but it was also making progress. While the paralyzed team was still trying to sort out the first step, the trusting team was already onto the third.

Now, you and your teams probably won't be defusing bombs as part of your everyday work (unless you work for a bomb squad, in which case, we salute you). Further, while you may work on deadlines, you rarely work on a five-minute timer—and usually, everyone in the team can't see what everyone else is doing.

But, time and again, this exercise illustrates the essential characteristics of successful and unsuccessful teams. The successful teams trust each other in all directions, often without question. They demonstrate empathy through listening, and they solve problems collaboratively. Their behaviors toward each other reveal their attitudes toward openness and create fast friendships out of strangers—all in under five minutes.

The unsuccessful teams, on the other hand, get hung up on process and tools, fear of failure, and power dynamics, rather than focusing on the common goal of making sure everyone in the room doesn't explode. Many teams with VP-level executives would literally freeze until the person with the most "power" made the first move. Even if they hadn't ever worked with the VP, they didn't want to make a bad impression—you know, for fear of squandering future career opportunities. Instead of playing the game, all their mental energy was diverted to keeping up appearances and playing a totally different game of politics with the boss.

This minute of silence is the same as a month of silence during the beginning of a large project. While everyone is trying to learn their own job and look good in front of the boss, no one is communicating. Then, for the next two or three months, no one takes any initiative. It's all back-and-forth messages and second-guessing. Before you know it, four months have gone by, and you only have one month left to complete five months of work.

When team members don't trust each other, the bomb explodes—whether figuratively or literally. In this chapter, we're going to teach you how to build expert, empathetic bomb squads. In other words, we're going to teach you how to create a high-performing team that is aligned with a culture of love.

THE FIVE TRAITS OF A HIGH-PERFORMING TEAM

First things first: if we're going to talk about how to build high-performing teams, then we need to be on the same page about what that means. After all, a lot of organizations (ours included) like to throw the term around, but it can often mean different things to different people.

In the simplest terms, a high-performing team is a team that regularly exceeds expectations. In our experience, this comes down to five key traits:

Autonomous. The members of high-performing teams are capable of working with limited outside oversight. They're able to collaborate and self-prioritize efficiently, and to link their work back to outcomes and goals.

Six-pillar culture. There's a high degree of openness, camaraderie, and trust. In fact, all of the Six Pillars are represented: inclusion, trust, empowerment, vulnerability, empathy, and forgiveness. Team members care for one another and hold one another accountable.

"We" is greater than "I." A high-performing individual on a low-performing team has little impact on the outcome. As we've said elsewhere in the book, it's better to have an all-star team than a team of all-stars. The members of high-performing teams are motivated to help each other, rather than motivated by self-interest. They pay attention to their teammates' needs and engage with empathy. If they are in competition, it's not against each other, but rather against forces outside the team or company.

Outcomes-oriented. Low- or average-performing teams tend to deliver only what is asked of them, even if they know better. Because they are more concerned with looking bad or embarrassing themselves, they focus on doing what they're told. A high-performing team, by contrast, delivers what is *needed*, not necessarily what is requested.

Fine with failure. Low-performing teams constantly worry about failure. High-performing teams see failure not as a destination, but as an opportunity to learn and improve. That's what a growth mindset looks like in action.

Do those traits describe your team or another team in your organization? If so, then you are probably part of a high-performing team—and that's something to celebrate! Many teams at Softway *thought* they were high-performing, but in reality, they were not. None of them thought they would fail when we first introduced the bomb game internally, and yet a majority of them did.

Ultimately, the difference comes down to risk tolerance. Risk-averse teams spend so much time feeding their fear that they get very little done. The fear of failure eats up more time than the failure itself. However, the teams that are willing to be vulnerable and openly share and discuss ideas with each other are naturally more willing to take risks because they have a sense of comfort and camaraderie. For the rest of this chapter, we're going to lay out the blueprint for success in your organization.

CREATE PSYCHOLOGICAL SAFETY

In Chapter 5, we shared the story of Amy Edmondson and her research on how working teams of doctors and nurses interacted. Much to her surprise, Edmondson found that the successfully performing teams were the ones that talked about their failures most often.

Edmondson also looked into the role of teamwork during the operation to rescue a group of thirty-three stranded Chilean miners in 2010. In order to get the trapped miners out, leaders assembled a diverse team of experts from several fields, including black ops, NASA astronauts, and geologists, among others. Despite their diverse backgrounds and expertise, the team communicated surprisingly well with each other. The geologist didn't pound on the table and insist she was right because she was the geologist. The special ops military person didn't insist he was right because he'd done more rescue missions than everyone else. Everyone was willing to add ideas together until they found the solution as a group.[7]

So what was their secret? Why were they able to communicate with each other and execute so effectively? In short, before setting out to solve the problem at hand, the team

---

7   Faaiza Rashid, Amy C. Edmondson, and Herman B. Leonard. "Leadership Lessons from the Chilean Mine Rescue." *Harvard Business Review.* July-August 2013. https://hbr.org/2013/07/leadership-lessons-from-the-chilean-mine-rescue

members worked to establish a sense of psychological safety. Each person understood they were there to solve the same problem—and that everyone's contribution to that problem was important and deserved to be heard. No one dominated the conversation, and everyone had a chance to contribute.

It may not seem like it at first glance, but your organization and the teams within it are composed of an equally diverse group of role players. You may not have geologists and astronauts working together, but your teams are likely to be composed of people with different needs and perspectives— such as project managers, analysts, engineers, and designers. The stakes may not be as high as defusing a bomb or rescuing a group of miners, but you still need to work together in order to reach your goal.

So how do you know you're creating a sense of psychological safety among your teams? Here are some traits to look out for:

Team members ask questions. If Chris was working on a project with us and there was something he didn't understand, he would ask. He's not afraid of being judged or criticized, so therefore he has no reason to keep his questions to himself. Further, he knows that by asking questions, he helps the team to consider all angles of a problem, anticipate problems, and improve their approach.

Team members engage others. If Jeff and Frank are trying to solve a problem and they notice Mohammad has disengaged, they don't shun him for not participating. They look for ways to help Mohammad get his mind back on the problem. Sometimes that means talking a problem out, and sometimes that means giving Mohammad some space for a moment. Either way, the solution starts by acknowledging the problem and stating your desire to move past it.

Team members forgive. It would have been easy for Jeff and Frank to get mad at Mohammad for checking out and let unforgiveness seep into their work. But Mohammad is only human, and no one can keep their head in the game 100 percent of the time. Speaking around problems doesn't solve anything. In fact, it considerably slows down progress. Forgiveness and reconciliation remove the sticky parts and get the team moving forward friction-free.

Every organization wants to create high-performing teams, but they ignore this critical first step. Instead, the person who has the most experience, the most seniority, or the most education commands an outsized influence on the problem-solving and decision-making process. This phenomenon is known as *intellectual arrogance,* and it usually leads to low-performing teams. Why? Because all those other people in the room who don't have the best job title or the most impressive degree are afraid to raise their hands and contribute—even if they're certain they know the answer to the problem. How much lived experience and wisdom could be translated into innovation in corporations, if only it were heard?

DESTROYING SAFETY

Psychological safety is often much easier to destroy than it is to create. Therefore, if you are focused on building psychological safety, don't be afraid to exercise authoritative power and call out any destructive behaviors quickly and unambiguously.

We've all seen the kinds of behaviors that alienate others: talking over other people, not inviting people to meetings they should be part of, spell-checking out loud, interrupting presentations, asking questions the person already knows the answers to, and so on. Manipulative and passive-aggressive misbehaviors are death to psychological safety (and a sure sign of a person playing mind games), and the marginalization these actions create cannot be tolerated.

Sometimes, psychologically unsafe behaviors are more overtly hostile. A team member might be using hostile, destructive language. Or, they might be approaching a problem with intellectual arrogance, ignoring others' suggestions simply because their education or job title doesn't "merit" the attention. Whatever the case, if you notice a behavior that is not conducive to a high-performing team, bring attention to it immediately by offering feedback or by practicing healthy authoritative power. Try not to respond with anger or hostility, but instead offer your feedback as a gift.

To take a more active role in a healthy working environment, download our pre-meeting psychological safety checklist at LoveAsABusiness Strategy.com.

COMMUNICATION AND EXPECTATIONS

What style of feedback should we use? How do we want to be held accountable? How should we discuss workload?

While effective expectation-setting means answering as many of these questions as you can upfront, it's never too late to take a moment and recenter. One of the benefits of an iterative approach (such as Agile; see Chapter 15) is to carve out time to make sure everyone understands and learns from each other. In this way, we establish working agreements—a defined series of statements that the team creates to hold themselves accountable and help everyone stay aligned.

At Softway we've chosen to use a direct style of communication in all situations. It's efficient and clear. Think about how Maggie communicated with Chris back in Chapter 1—directly and unambiguously. Sure, addressing the issue head-on meant Chris felt a little sheepish for the next few days, but it also brought Maggie's concerns out into the open rather than letting them fester.

We would argue that this approach to communication is the standard to which all teams should aspire. When defusing imaginary bombs, there's simply no time for fluff. Open and honest conversations allow our teams to align, provide us with a blueprint for how to resolve disputes before they happen, and help us solve problems collaboratively.

Do not mistake directness for cruelty. The particular way we communicate at Softway might be effective for us, but it might fall flat in other organizations. Instead, think of these discussions as a positive prenup. In any group of people, there will always be something that goes wrong. Having an honest discussion with the team can set expectations and make that issue much easier when it does arise.

ACCOUNTABILITY

Often, when people hear the word accountability, they get nervous. They think of accountability in terms of deliverables. Did they get that assignment in on time? Did they remember to send off that email? Did they get the order for the team lunch right?

To be fair, this *is* what accountability looks like in low-performing teams. This form of accountability is rooted in authoritative and punitive power, as well as an awareness of hierarchy. But if this kind of accountability doesn't work in low-performing teams, it certainly won't work in a culture of love. When we think of accountability in a high-performing team, here's what we mean:

> Stand with your teammates—for them, with them, alongside them. Whatever they do, you do.

> Uphold high standards of performance and expectations so that everyone can achieve them.

> Speak up, even if you're disappointed or frustrated.

> Don't offer feedback as a personal attack, but rather as an invitation to help the team improve.

To understand what accountability in a culture of love looks like, think back to how Maggie held Chris accountable for missing their one-on-ones, or how Frank held Mohammad accountable for yelling at him for a meeting he knew nothing about. In each instance, both Frank and Maggie were certainly frustrated (among other strong feelings), but they communicated that frustration and held their team members accountable in a way that invited improvement rather than stoked conflict.

GIVING FEEDBACK

Imagine Jeff has just handed you a gift—or at least, he said it was a gift. In reality, it looks like trash. The box is wrapped in newspaper with strips of randomly-colored duct tape—topped off with a little bit of twine that is apparently supposed to be a bow. You take Jeff's gift, thank him for being so thoughtful, and then set it down without opening it. *Whatever that is, it can wait,* you say to yourself.

Then Chris hands you a gift. It looks and feels amazing—nice, shiny paper perfectly tucked and folded as it should be and six-inch ribbon curls trailing down like icing on a cake. It looks as if he paid someone to wrap it for him, but he smiles and says he did it himself. Impressed, you open Chris's gift right away and look inside to find your favorite new card game: Throw Throw Burrito. (Look it up. It's a real game, and it's fantastic.)

Now you turn back to Jeff's gift and sigh. *Well, I guess I'll have to open it,* you say to yourself, *but if a squirrel or something jumps out at me, I'm going to freaking lose it.* You unlace the twine, peel off a strip of duct tape, and unwrap the newspaper to find...another copy of Throw Throw Burrito.

Would you look at that? Two wildly different wrapping jobs. *Exactly the same gift.*

Giving feedback is a lot like giving a gift: you can wrap it up however you like, but the only thing that matters is what's inside. Sure, when someone offers you feedback, you might be a little more receptive if it's wrapped up nicely, but if not, you still got something incredibly valuable—the gift of someone else's perspective.

At Softway, we're big gift-givers—both in terms of actual gifts (as in the story of Mohammad's stuffed luggage in Chapter

10), and the gift of feedback. Because we love each other and care about everyone's success, we want to give them the best opportunity to succeed. Besides, giving feedback is inevitable. We're all human. Eventually, you or a teammate will misbehave or fall short of expectations, and you're going to have a hard conversation. But while these may be hard conversations, they're also incredibly valuable—and if your team is built on a strong foundation of psychological safety, you will feel safe both giving and receiving essential feedback. Moreover, you will see the difference that feedback has on your team's performance.

Let's say you have two identical teams. One team has a free flow of feedback between everyone from the team leader to the junior member and vice versa. Titles and roles don't matter; one human being can teach another human being. Mistakes are discussed, and lessons are learned. Everyone is a good gift-giver, even going so far as to practice the Platinum Rule and learn how to wrap feedback in a way that's easy to unwrap and apply.

The other team, in contrast, is afraid to give any feedback. They suck at giving gifts. Team members aren't able to fully understand their mistakes, pivot, or learn. They're afraid of criticizing the leaders, and the leaders are afraid of hurting anyone's feelings. Everyone is afraid of looking bad in front of their teammates, but no one has a clear idea of their own strengths and weaknesses.

Over time, the team that gives good gifts improves much quicker and much more significantly than the team that doesn't. They learn. They grow. They talk about mistakes so frequently that feedback stops even being stressful. It stops being an "event." As a result, everyone on the team improves. By communicating freely, they *learned* freely as well.

Meanwhile, the other team stays essentially the same, making only incremental gains at best. Even worse, the act of giving and receiving feedback is a big production. The person giving the feedback has to carefully consider how they will deliver their message, walking on eggshells the entire time. Meanwhile, the person receiving the feedback dreads the experience, walks in anxious and stressed out, and resents the entire exchange afterward. What a nightmare.

This is what happens when teams get too caught up in *how* the gift is wrapped rather than *what's inside*—they toss it in the trash without even peeking. What would opening the gift have even looked like? How could it have affected how you approached your work? Even if you disagree with what's being said, that person is giving you an opportunity to see another perspective or angle. After all, there's always something to learn.

If you want to be a Chris-level gift wrapper (six-inch ribbon curls are *not* impossible), then the best way to start is by practicing the Platinum Rule. But the truth is, if you have a solid relationship, the person who received the gift should be able to look past a bad wrapping job and see the value in what you have to say. Of course, this asks the question: How do you know whether you're giving good feedback?

HOW TO GIVE BAD FEEDBACK

You've just kicked off in a one-on-one meeting with Frank. Before you dive into the conversation, Frank says, "Hey, just so you know, you had spinach in your teeth all day yesterday."

"Thanks?" you say, unsure what good the information will do you now. You know that Frank was just trying to be nice, but it sure would have been more helpful if he'd told you that yesterday.

You probably get the point of this story. Good feedback is actionable; bad feedback is not. To avoid your own Frank moment, give your feedback as close to real time as possible. Don't wait for the perfect situation. Don't curate the perfect playlist, light the candles, and set the mood. The longer you wait, the less relevant the feedback becomes, and the less opportunity the person has to learn. Besides, the sooner you give the feedback, the sooner it's over with—which means a lot less stress for you.

Untimely feedback isn't the only way to give bad feedback, of course. Here are a few other things to avoid:

Unfounded gossip. Just because you heard Peter was having trouble with his TPS reports doesn't make it true. Before offering any feedback, make sure you have your facts straight.

Playing the messenger. Here's a sure sign you're giving bad feedback: "Hey, I just wanted you to know—and it's not me saying this—but Mohammad was saying that he's tired of the 'science project'—his words—that you left in the refrigerator. Do you think you can do something about that?" If you're giving feedback, it needs to come from you. Don't hide behind someone else's feedback in order to give your own.

A chance to misbehave. As it turns out, you never did have spinach in your teeth the other day. Frank was just saying that to mess with you. (That's *so* shady, Frank!) If your goal in giving feedback isn't to help someone, but rather to attack, belittle, or play mind games with that person, then it's a good bet you're not offering any good feedback.

There are other ways to give bad feedback—too many to list in this book. But here's the big picture: if you're not sure how to deliver feedback, start with one of our Principles of Servant Leadership—assume good intent.

HOW TO GIVE GOOD FEEDBACK

We were in a client meeting, about to make a pivotal decision, when our client pushed back hard. Suddenly, all the air went out of the room, and Mohammad shut down. Any sense of momentum we had quickly ground to a halt.

Up to that point, Frank had been on the sidelines, typing away on his laptop. But as the silence grew more awkward and the side conversations grew annoyed, Frank realized he had to make a decision: address the situation and offer some constructive feedback to get the conversation rolling or let the awkwardness continue.

Frank knew what he *wanted* to do. He was perfectly happy sitting there in front of his laptop, thank you very much, and he had sometimes been fearful of giving feedback in the past (remember the story of the missed meeting in Chapter 3?). However, he also knew that they were there to serve their client—and right now, they weren't doing it.

After taking a few more moments to assess the situation, Frank concluded that no one else was going to speak up. It was up to him. So, he closed his laptop, cleared his throat, and spoke.

"I want everybody to stop for a quick minute, please."

Everyone in the room stopped what they were doing and turned their attention to Frank. He continued.

"Mohammad, I noticed that you shut down in the conversation just now, and that cannot happen. We're at a pivotal moment in time. What can we do to bring you back into the conversation and help us make this decision?"

Instead of giving the feedback later—or even offering it one-on-one away from the client—Frank chose to address the issue immediately. However, Frank knew that either of those approaches would create a worse experience for everyone in the room—especially their clients, who were literally paying to be there.

This approach wasn't without risks, of course. Mohammad could have responded negatively after Frank called attention to him. However, Mohammad knew that Frank wasn't calling him out just to call him out. Frank *hates* confrontation and would only do something like this if he was truly trying to help his teammate. Even more, Frank had done something crucially important to give good feedback: he focused on finding a path forward by directly asking Mohammad what he needed to re-engage in the conversation. He offered a gift of feedback that was actionable rather than a critique. As a result, Mohammad was able to get clarity on what was bothering him and what was needed, and therefore he was able to rejoin the conversation. After everyone in the room took a moment to get on the same page, Mohammad did indeed feel re-engaged, and he was able to move through the rest of his presentation without a hitch.

Offering feedback in the moment can often feel awkward, especially in a group setting. But often, as was the case in this situation, things were awkward already. Better to lean into the awkwardness, call it out, and work to resolve it than to let it fester indefinitely, which could eventually lead to unforgiveness. By creating an opportunity for everyone to move past the awkwardness, the team was able to come back together around a shared goal and continue to move forward.

FOCUS ON A PATH TO ACTION

Imagine if one of your teammates walked up to you and said that you were hard to talk to during meetings. How would you feel? Probably not great—and you'd probably have no sense of how to improve your behaviors in that situation, either.

In moments like that, the gift of feedback is all wrapping and no present. Even worse, it's not a particularly good wrapping job.

If you want to make sure you actually included a present with your gift, be sure to include clear, actionable feedback. Even if you don't wrap the present very well, most of the time your teammates will recognize the offering and thank you for it.

That said, if you can, take care to wrap your feedback as well as you can. Follow the Platinum Rule. Take a moment to understand what your teammate needs and how you can best help them get there.

THE ROLE OF LEADERS ON A HIGH-PERFORMING TEAM

In the bomb game, if you screw up and clip the wrong wire, there are no real consequences. In business, setting off a figurative bomb could have far-reaching consequences for your organization. But whether in the bomb game or at work, mistakes are going to happen. The question is, how do you and your team react afterward? Do you watch as your team shuts down and everyone around you flies into a panic? Or, does someone step in to pick you up, reorient the team, and keep pushing ahead?

This is what a culture of love looks like in action—engaged team members working together to focus on the task at hand and get things done even as they're racing against the clock and staring down near-impossible odds. But great teams require great leaders—someone who can assess the situation, provide resources, and create an environment of psychological safety for their teams to thrive.

This is where servant leadership comes in. To put it mildly, prior to 2016, Softway's leaders weren't exactly great at fostering psychological safety, offering feedback, or otherwise supporting their teams. Letters about refrigerator etiquette were the norm rather than the exception. Unsurprisingly, that harsh feedback style made its way through the organization; if the CEO saw that as acceptable behavior, then others felt empowered to behave the same way.

Once Mohammad embraced love and began working to change his own feedback style, he realized that changing himself wasn't enough to fix the feedback problem. If he couldn't get other leaders—and ultimately, every single role-player on every single team—to buy into love-based communication strategies, then his own efforts would only get him so far.

This led to some soul searching. How could we encourage

leaders to adopt our Six Pillars of Love in how they managed, coached, and gave feedback to their teams? Moreover, if the goal of building high-functioning teams was to encourage autonomy, then what did the leader's role even look like? Here is how we see the leader's role in a high-functioning team:

Create the vision and goals. Do you have a vision for what the team or the organization is doing? Are everyone's goals aligned with that vision? No meaningful progress can happen without it.

Establish the identity and mission. The leader creates the identity and mission of each team. The team should understand the reason why they exist.

Set expectations and facilitate conversations. The leader facilitates the team's conversations around working agreements and norms. How will the team communicate? Does everyone understand the expectations? The leader helps create alignment in the group, but also adds to the discussion.

Focus on results. Naturally, to have a high-performing team, you have to perform. This doesn't just mean throwing time at a problem—eighty hours spent with no clear results are eighty hours wasted. Help team members look practically at what they're trying to accomplish and how they can maximize their time and resources.

Generate psychological safety. Have you ever had so much fun working on a project that coming to work and throwing down with your teammates was the best part of your day? Love-focused leaders are always working to make work feel exciting and meaningful. When team members trust each other, when they enjoy the work and *want* to be around each other, that's where the magic happens.

These are essential traits of any leader on a high-performing team. However, let's be clear: leaders cannot change team culture on their own. The behaviors we identified here begin with the leader, but every individual team member must learn to embrace these behaviors if their culture of love is going to thrive. Everyone is responsible for the team or the organization's culture. Every team member is responsible for their own transformation. Each of us can support and empower each other on our journeys.

In fact, if enough individuals operate with the right behaviors and attitudes, the culture will change regardless of the leader. That's how the best teams work. The individuals within the team treat each other with the right behaviors, and it strengthens the capability and performance of everyone on that team. Just as misbehaviors build on themselves, so do positive behaviors. The more team members see others supporting each other, offering feedback, holding each other accountable, and pushing each other to perform at their best, the more they are inclined to adopt those same behaviors themselves.

DOING YOUR PART

As we get ready to push on to the next chapter, we return to a question we posed earlier in the book: how do you change the culture of an organization with hundreds, thousands, maybe even tens of thousands of employees?

The answer: you don't.

Instead, you change your own behaviors first. Your behavior is your responsibility. Whether you're behaving or misbehaving—whether you're building or destroying a culture of love—that behavior is contagious.

At some point in your career, you've probably had to work with someone with a prickly personality, someone with a fixed mindset who saw every new challenge as an insurmountable problem. How did you receive this person? Did the apathy and disassociation kick in as you sought ways to work around this person? Or, did you examine your own behaviors with that teammate and look for a better way forward?

None of us should be defined by our own worst traits and tendencies. Each of us can learn how to behave actively and collaboratively as part of a high-functioning team. Sometimes, we just need someone to show us the way, to invite us in, and to remind us that our contributions matter too. In the next chapter, we'll explore all the many ways to do just that.

CHAPTER 12

HR (HUMANITY REQUIRED)

Chris thought he had the good fortune of joining an up-and-coming company like Softway in 2015—right before we entered our downturn and less than one month before we laid off a hundred team members and pivoted to a culture of love as a business strategy.

It goes without saying, then, that the Softway Chris would come to know and love was not the Softway that greeted him on his first day.

As Chris walked through the lobby on his first day of work, no one was there to greet him—and he had no idea where to go. As he stopped at a fork in the hallway, a distracted Mohammad almost ran right into him.

"Oh! You're starting today. I'd forgotten." Mohammad smiled, but he was clearly stressed. "I'm sorry, I don't have any time for you today, but you can go see our HR director and she'll get you squared away."

Okay, but where was HR? Was the HR director even expecting him?

Chris continued his aimless search through Softway's halls. Finally, he found the HR director, grabbed a seat, and began filling out paperwork.

Chris had no idea what he was supposed to do next and it was clear that the HR director didn't either.

She looked at Chris. Chris looked back awkwardly.

"Do you have any questions about Softway before you go to your desk?" she finally asked.

Chris shifted in his chair. "Um. Well. I can tell you what I know. If I'm missing anything, maybe you can fill in the gaps for me." She agreed. He talked for about ten minutes, and as he did, her eyes got wider and wider. In the end, she looked at him and said, "Oh, wow. You know more than I do."

How strange.

By now, Chris was starting to get antsy. In less than two hours on his first day, the CEO had blown him off, and HR clearly didn't know what to do with him. But, since he was here, he might as well go to his desk.

Chris found his office and glanced down at his desk to find a solitary laptop with a sticky note attached to the top. On it was his username and password. But there was just one problem: his username was spelled wrong, and his password didn't work. He couldn't log in. Time for another trip around the office!

Eventually, Chris found someone who could help him. "Hi, I'm told you're in charge of laptops. Two things. I started today, and my name's misspelled and I can't log into the laptop."

The team member stared back at Chris. "Do you want me to change the spelling, or are you okay with keeping it?" he said, clearly hoping for the latter.

Chris didn't want to sound like a jerk—especially not on his first day. But he also wanted his name spelled correctly on his company login. Finally, he thought up a diplomatic solution. "Yes, my email address should reflect the accurate spelling of my name. I'd hate for a client to get confused and for me to not get an email if they spelled it correctly. So, yes, please. I also need to be able to log in."

The team member took the laptop. Chris stood around—literally twiddling his thumbs—before finally going back to his desk. New team members walked past the office. Chris would wave, the team members would wave back, and then they would be on their way. No one stopped to say hi. No one asked what he was doing (literally nothing) or whether they could help show him around. Eventually, he packed up his stuff and headed home.

Worst. First. Day. Ever. (Okay, maybe second-worst. At least Chris didn't have to assemble his $60 desk and $29 chair on his first day as Jeff did. But that's another story for another time.)

Surprisingly, Chris came back the next day. And the day after that. And the day after that. And we're lucky he did. We're even luckier that after that horrible, rotten, no-good day, Chris vowed that no one at Softway would ever have a first-day experience like that again.

As easy as it is to look back and laugh at how bad that initial experience was, first impressions matter—a lot. In fact, research shows that a person's first ninety days at a new company will determine whether they feel at home the rest of their time there.[8] How you recruit, how you hire, and how you manage and grow your talent matters. After all, in a culture of love, people are the whole point.

And yet, like the old Softway, many organizations treat these processes almost as an afterthought. They outsource and automate recruiting tasks using third-party providers. They use software to scan resumes for certain keywords and return only those with the closest matches.

Not only do these practices tend to marginalize people, but they also limit a hiring manager's options. They reflect the organization's bias toward what the right candidate would look like, and in so doing, they exclude many qualified candidates who don't match that picture.

Again, this used to be us too. We used to have a stringent checklist for the resumes received, all based on our picture of what candidates for given roles should look like. Unfortunately, when we leaned too much on cookie-cutter resumes,

---

8   Arlene S. Hirsch, "Don't Underestimate the Importance of Good Onboarding," SHRM, August 10, 2017, https://www.shrm.org/resourcesandtools/hr-topics/talent-acquisition/pages/dont-underestimate-the-importance-of-effective-onboarding.aspx.

we missed candidates whose life experiences might have better suited the roles we needed to fill. We were optimizing for keywords and not the ability to solve challenges or connect with teams. There was no humanity at all in the way we hired humans.

As we started to transform into a culture of love, we worked to apply those principles to every step of the talent management journey—from recruiting and hiring, to managing and promoting. Our goal? To infuse the process with humanity, to identify the key traits of our candidates' personalities, and to ask ourselves not just whether they'd be good for the job, but whether they'd be good for a culture of love. Would we actually want to hang out with this person? Would we want to sit next to them? What difference would they bring to our ways of solving problems? Could we count on them to do the work?

Checking a box that said someone had three years of experience and a certification didn't get us what we really wanted. But maybe learning about who these people were and how we could best serve each other might. In the following sections, we'll share the story of that journey, and what we learned along the way.

HIRING FOR SUCCESS

Have you ever received a detailed agenda and comprehensive instructions on what to expect ahead of an interview? Softway candidates do. The day before their interview, a recruiter calls the candidate and tells them everything they can expect. The candidate learns about each leader and team member they will be interviewing with—including their personality, their interview style, and their pet peeves.

For instance, if the candidate is interviewing with Jeff, the recruiter tells them that Jeff likes to give people little puzzles to see how they solve problems. Or, if the candidate is interviewing with Mohammad, the recruiter tells them that Mohammad loves punctuality—and talking about University of Houston football. Whatever information we think might help the candidate succeed, we make sure they know.

To be clear, our recruiters don't share this information as a test. Rather, our recruiters see themselves as advocates for our candidates. If there's going to be an on-the-spot test, we want them to be mentally prepared for that so they can represent their best versions of themselves.

Additionally, we take a team approach to the interviews, rather than relying on a single hiring manager. This is for our benefit as much as theirs. After all, we want the relevant teams to actually meet the candidates who might eventually work with them. During the interview process, many organizations try to trip up job candidates to see how they react. They ask hardball questions, interrupt the candidates' answers, and challenge them constantly. Ostensibly, they use tactics like this to see how a candidate might respond in front of a client. We see no use for this—no client of ours would even behave that way.

Rather than trying to stress our candidates, we introduce interviews as a series of friendly chats. We try to make the candidate comfortable and feel as if they belong. The reasoning behind this is simple: if the candidate feels welcome at Softway but we don't extend an offer, the worst outcome is that the person applies again. If they had an issue or weren't the right fit, we will tell them and encourage them to find the right opportunity. Perhaps they will find it with us someday.

Once the interviews have concluded, the entire team gets together to learn how the interaction went. We check to see whether anyone felt marginalized or uncomfortable at any point in the conversation. (You'd be surprised how many candidates never make eye contact with a particular person.) In this way, we ensure that any new hire adds to the culture and models inclusive behaviors.

This screening process works both ways: if someone is coming in to interview for a job, they're judging us too—and rightfully so. We want candidates to meet the teams they'd be working with, and to be put at ease. Not only will the experience be easier for them, but we will be able to better understand who they are and what they can contribute if they're not stressed out.

Often, other HR leaders have a lot of questions about our approach. Why spend so much effort on all those detailed instructions? For us, the answer is simple: it shows us who the candidates are! If someone can't follow directions now, they won't suddenly learn on the job. If they're arrogant to a lowly recruiter, they will also be arrogant on the job. Our process separates those who can learn and be coached from those who can't, those who will fit in with our unique culture from those who won't. As a result, we've successfully identified and hired candidates who would have fallen through the cracks of a traditional recruiting and hiring process.

FINDING THE RIGHT PEOPLE

Branden hadn't had an easy life. At fifteen he was homeless. By twenty-one, he was at the end of his rope, toiling away at a startup for months on end without getting paid. In fact, the startup was costing *him* money by running up expenses on his credit card. On top of that, he had a serious medical condition with no health insurance to treat it, and he could barely afford to eat.

This was the Branden we met when he applied for the role of designer, though none of us knew it at the time. All we knew was that he had talent, enthusiasm, and a gentle way about him. We liked this combination of traits, and we liked the range of experience he brought to the table. So while the designer role wasn't a good fit for him, we asked him to interview for the project coordinator role instead. He accepted, and from there he soared through his interviews.

Not only were we taken with Branden, but he was taken with us as well. In fact, after walking out of his interview that day, Branden made a pact with himself: no applying or interviewing for any other jobs until he heard a no from Softway.

He nearly fainted when we called to offer him the job.

Fast forward a couple of years later, and now Branden is one of our high-performing employees. He regularly goes above and beyond for us because he feels we took a chance on a kid that was one step away from ending up back on the streets. The value of team members like Branden cannot be overstated. After all, Softway isn't the biggest company in the pond. Our office isn't the most impressive-looking, and we haven't won as many awards as some other organizations.

Still, we consistently attract great talent like Branden because of our recruiting and interviewing practices. Softway candidates never forget how they were treated. They never forget that they were included from day one and given all the tools they needed to succeed. They never forget that we've given them a chance that no one else would. In turn, they respond with incredible work, dedication, and passion.

HIRING WITH LOVE = MORE DIVERSE TEAMS

Our hiring process hasn't just been good for finding incredible talent. It has also led to more diverse hiring practices. In the past, we often made the mistake of hiring only people like ourselves. New recruits usually had similar levels of education, had similar skills, talked like us, and otherwise reminded us of ourselves in a number of ways. Such hiring practices might have been good for the ego, but we unconsciously denied ourselves a diversity of talent.

Moreover, that hiring practice was limiting our growth. Softway already employed people who thought like us—adding more of them didn't help us innovate or create better systems and processes. It took a wider variety of perspectives to do that.

Once we began pursuing love as a recruiting strategy, our workforce began to grow more diverse over time. Today, we have people from different ethnicities, different economic and educational backgrounds, and from different parts of the world—and we've seen that diversity lead directly to innovation and growth.

At the core of our approach is our ability to look beyond the resume to see the real person. We're careful to consider people with nonstandard backgrounds for a given role, rather than only hire people who have been in similar positions. We care more about someone's ability to do the job than what their background looks like on paper.

Don't recruit as if you were painting by numbers. Be open to what someone's background and life experience might bring to the table.

A RAISE ON THE SPOT

Softway once had a rigid performance management system, particularly in our India office. We asked for a personal assessment, provided a manager's assessment, filled in the rest of the information using a rubric, and then used all this information to calculate a person's raise for the year. We made these assessments once per year, and it was a stressful experience for everyone. Many employees were underwhelmed with the raise they received.

The system was set up so that a team member's reviewing manager was not the person overseeing their projects. We thought it was a good idea at the time, but the result was that no manager could accurately assess performance. Some reviewing managers were put in charge of people based on discipline or function, and may not have seen the team member's work at all. The system was designed to be data-driven and unbiased, but in practice, it ended up rewarding favorites. It gave the most money to the people who happened to stay with the company the longest.

As a result, the annual conversation became what we call a "fish market negotiation." The manager would say that the company was prepared to give the team member X amount of money. The team member would respond that they were expecting more, knowing full well this was their only chance to negotiate for the year. The managers, meanwhile, weren't particularly interested in the negotiations. All they wanted out of the evaluations was to reward their favorite team members and retaliate against the ones they didn't like.

Even worse, the system didn't result in any real conversations about performance. No one got feedback until their annual review on the anniversary of their hiring, and in practice they didn't even get an actual performance review then. The conversation jumped quickly to appraisal and then negotiation.

Our approach wasn't unusual. We modeled our system after big corporations—and we got big corporate results. However, while our performance management process may have felt stable and predictable, our talent wasn't growing their skillsets. The great team members left when they didn't get the pay raise they deserved, while the team members who stayed learned to play the system rather than work on their skills.

During our transition to a culture of love, we came across an article about an organization that practiced what they called "spot raises." According to the article, this organization bucked the idea of withholding pay and feedback during the year. If a person did great work, they deserved a raise—whether that was every week, every two months, or every two years. Perform, and you'd get rewarded.

We decided to bring that radical idea to our own organization, creating a similar system that rewarded people for good work on the spot. In this new system, team members were no longer guaranteed a raise every year. Instead, they would be rewarded based on their performance. We set up ways to measure performance for different roles, which often had nothing to do with bill-ability. And then we rolled it out.

At first, some team members were uncomfortable with this new system. They'd been used to getting their raise every year, and they didn't like all this talk about "earning it." Then they saw the new system in action. The hard workers, in particular, embraced the new system, excited that they could now influence their own pay in a direct and powerful way, earning rewards not only for their performance, but also for growing their skillsets.

Overall, this new system has been wildly effective. No longer did conversations about raises seem like fish market negotiations. Instead, they became a surprise affirmation of excellent work. You did something that was worth recognizing, and you were appreciative and grateful it was noticed. When it comes down to it, frequent feedback and rewards without delay are inherently motivating. In fact, even when pay is decoupled from the conversation, feedback still leads to growth, and team members still take on challenges they wouldn't have touched otherwise. But the spot raises still matter. They're our way of reaffirming that we value our people, that we value their work, and that we are invested in their growth.

AGILE TALENT MANAGEMENT

Around the same time we were altering our performance management system, we also reorganized so that leaders could build real relationships with their direct reports. To do that, we built cross-functional teams oriented around a specific project or type of project. The leader who oversaw the team could therefore also see the work they created. These practices reflect what is known as an *Agile* methodology (see Chapter 15 for the full story of how we went Agile).

While cross-functional teams reflect our commitment to adopting Agile processes in our organization, they can also complicate career paths. In a typical organization, as a person builds an increasingly specialized skillset, their career trajectory tends to move in a straight line. In Agile teams, people tend to develop instead as deep generalists, with specific expertise in one area and general skills in others. This T-shaped skillset creates more options for both the team and team members, building resilience for both. That said, it also removes linear career paths.

Here's why. Instead of a managerial role, teams have two key roles: facilitator and leader. The leadership role is specific to that team, and therefore it can be filled by anyone. It doesn't require management experience. You can move into a leadership role without giving up your day-to-day, hands-on work, and you can become more senior without becoming a leader. This team-based system allows people to grow into adjacent skillsets.

At the beginning of this shift to Agile processes, many team members pushed back. The change didn't feel natural. But once people saw the flexibility it gave them in their work—a designer could tackle copywriting, a coder could be a project manager—they saw how effective this approach was in breaking down silos and removing barriers to getting work done. No longer did team members have to wait for the "expert" to become available in order to do a basic thing. Instead, anyone could step in to fill needs as they identified them.

Teams can come together and tackle any challenge they're given. The more psychological safety they build, and the better their teamwork, the more they're able to accomplish.

As successful as these Agile teams have been, because of their nature, they can sometimes lead to a sense of ambiguity. By empowering team members to wear different hats, weren't we also pushing them off their career paths? This is a valid question, but in our experience, this hasn't been the case. A graphic designer who steps in to do a little copywriting is still a graphic designer and still on that path. But now, they've expanded their skillset and become more competent in their job in ways that they otherwise wouldn't have considered. By offering our team members new ways of working and new approaches to problem-solving, our team members have *more* options for their careers, not fewer.

PROMOTIONAL EQUITY

In organizations with diverse talent, people from non-dominant groups are typically promoted more slowly than people from dominant groups. People from non-dominant groups begin to feel they won't be able to realize their potential within the organization, and they leave. Unfortunately, that reinforces the notion internally that non-dominant groups are not capable of delivering outcomes. That negative bias infiltrates performance management, recruiting, onboarding, training, and development. It perpetuates itself, becoming a self-fulfilling prophecy.

When you have love as a business strategy, on the other hand, you're committed to realizing the potential in everyone. You're committed to building relationships, trust, empowering people, and all the other pillars, not for just one person on your team but for everyone. If you're doing this correctly, everyone should see the opportunity to earn promotions within the organization.

EVERY DAY SHOULD FEEL LIKE FRIDAY

Embracing love as a business strategy forced us to rethink every aspect of our recruiting, hiring, onboarding, and management processes. We've come a long way since Chris's worst first day ever.

These days, every Softway team member's first day is always a Friday. From the moment they arrive, they're greeted personally and taken to their desk—where a basket of treats awaits. Because we got to know our new hires during the interview process, the treats are hand-picked to match their tastes. (For instance, when we learned another new team member had a thing for chocolate glazed donuts, we made sure he had as many as he could eat on his first day.)

From there, every new hire has a jam-packed agenda full of welcome meetings. Through the course of these meetings, they'll meet their new team, their supervisor, and anyone else they will be working with on a regular basis. Afterward, the new hire is then introduced to the company during our Friday standup meeting, where we like to keep it loose and fun. Then, we send them out for lunch with their team. No one eats alone on their first day! For the rest of the day, we set up meetings across the organization over the next few weeks. New hires quickly get up to speed with their closest contacts, and then they get the chance to meet people outside of their team.

And then they're done—and ready to enjoy the weekend. In our view, this is the best possible introduction. After all, there's nothing like getting two days off for one day of work!

Making our team members feel welcome and included from the moment they set foot in the door isn't just good for morale. It's good for business. In fact, as we'll see in the next chapter, it's the key driver of our business outcomes.

CHAPTER 13

SYSTEMS: PEOPLE, PROCESS, AND TECHNOLOGY

Before our transformation to a culture of love, Softway suffered from systemic mistrust. Our policies, systems, and technology choices all reflected that. We thought we were doing the right things, creating processes that people told us would improve the business. However, in the name of efficiency, we were creating harm and holding our team back. Worse, it didn't even work. We created inefficiency in the name of efficiency, doing harm along the way.

Nowhere was this more evident than in our choice to install a biometric tracking system in our Bengaluru, India, office. This thumbprint-based system allowed us to record the comings and goings of all our team members. We knew exactly when someone arrived at work and when they left.

We told our team members that this system was purely for security and confidentiality. But in practice, we used it to punish tardy employees. If we did not have a team member's fingerprint in our system by eleven in the morning, we docked their pay and instructed HR to begin calling them to come into work. When the team member finally did show up, they would not be paid for the day until HR formally excused them.

Not only was this system both dehumanizing and marginalizing (notice how we didn't install the same system in our Houston, Texas, office), it was also inefficient. As we learned from Sunil's story in Chapter 8, tracking down tardy team members took a lot of work—literally HR's entire morning. This was time taken away from what we actually wanted them to do: recruit prospective employees and otherwise manage the screening, hiring, and talent development processes. Because they had to spend their mornings dealing with lateness, they constantly took flak from their direct managers, who didn't understand why so little progress was being made. HR understood the problem all too well, but they were powerless to do anything about it.

Sunil and the rest of the HR team weren't the only ones trapped in a hell they couldn't escape. No one was happy with the new tracking system. And eventually, this dissatisfaction led to exactly the opposite results we'd expected to see. *More* team members began showing up to work late—if at all. They didn't appreciate the calls from HR and the unexpected pay cuts. They felt as if they were constantly being punished by angry parents. The more they felt this way, the less they wanted to work.

This vicious cycle would even follow team members on vacation. If someone went on leave for four or five days without formally applying for vacation, the system would mark them as absent, and as a result we would dock their pay. Even worse, we wouldn't tell them about it in advance. Team members would get their paychecks at the end of the month only to find there was only a third of what they were expecting.

These team members were perfectly eligible to go on leave and had cleared it with their managers and team members. No one was cheating the system. They had just forgotten to formally submit their request. And yet, in this punitive, distrusting culture, we had created unnecessary obstacles for them to get paid what they deserved. In fact, even after they discovered the problem, it was up to them to do something about it; to get the money they were due, first they had to prove to HR and management that they'd gone on a genuine, sanctioned vacation. Then, they had to get their manager to follow another set of protocols to vouch for them. If the manager failed to do *their* part, then the employee's pay was still docked.

At the risk of stating the obvious, docking employees' pay—especially without telling them—is antithetical to a culture of love. These policies actively harmed our team members. As a result of our greedy, mistrustful practices, many employees weren't able to make ends meet. They missed car payments and medical bills. They struggled to feed their families. All because they'd forgotten to fill out a form—and because we were too beholden to our systems to make the process any easier for them.

To be clear, this wasn't a tech issue. The biometric scanners weren't the problem. (Technology in itself is neither good nor evil. It is just a tool.) The problem was the rampant mistrust baked into the very fabric of our culture. We lacked the trust, empathy, and compassion necessary for a culture of love to thrive and instead fostered only a culture of fear.

Here again, Softway was no different from many companies. Leaders often turn to processes and technology in the name of efficiency and innovation. They may mean well by these initiatives, but approached from the wrong mindset, the results are often the opposite of what they expected.

These days, it doesn't matter how technical the process or mundane the system. Every policy decision we make is approached through a lens of love. We're constantly asking how our decisions and interactions impact others. If our systems don't reflect our desire to put people first, then our claim to have a culture of love would be meaningless.

As for the biometric scanners, they had cost a lot of money, but we decided to stop using them...mostly. These days, we only use them for after-hours security. This helps our team members feel safer if they're working late and provides us with some extra protection when no one else is there. Here, the intention is everything. Instead of using these scanners as a tool of distrust, we use them to reflect our investment in the physical and mental well-being of each and every team member. This people-first mindset now drives every process and tool we adopt. As a result, not only do our team members trust us again, but our productivity has skyrocketed.

In this chapter, we're going to talk about how to view your systems in a culture of love. To do that, instead of looking at each area of your business one by one (e.g., operations, sales, and marketing), we're going to keep our focus on a common thread running through every part of your organization: people. When you focus on how you can best support your people, all decisions on processes and tools will flow naturally from there.

PROCESS ISN'T THE WAY OUT

When faced with challenges, most businesses try to solve them by adding in more processes. For years, we were no different. Our executive leadership team of industry vets had convinced us that process was the way forward, and we weren't about to argue.

And yet for every new bit of process we added, our results didn't change. Sales didn't improve. Engagement didn't increase. If anything, our results got worse. Communication among departments was nonexistent. Project management was a mess. Employee absenteeism—which our biometric scanners made us acutely aware of—was a chronic problem. Whatever the specifics, whatever the department, our approach to the problem was always the same: we looked at the process again, added more steps, and demanded that our teams follow each one to the letter.

These processes looked sound on paper. In application, however, all we had built was a pressure cooker. As team members fell further and further behind, we put up more and more barriers to execution. We were constantly complaining about our team members not showing up on time (or failing to show up at all). All they had to do was follow the process we had laid out for them. Was that really so hard?

In fact, it was. We couldn't see how we were setting our team members up for failure back then—and how mistrust in one area caused a chain reaction of problems in others. In fact, it took a brave act on the part of Sunil to bring the issue to our attention. But we can see the issue clearly now. We were so focused on process and tech adoption that we forgot that real, living and breathing people did the work. We had no idea what kind of environment we were creating for our team members—and as a result, we had no empathy for the work we were asking them to do.

By withholding empathy, we also disempowered our entire organization. How can you take ownership of your work or take pride in what you do if your every move is scrutinized, catalogued, and reported? What incentive do you have to innovate when you live in fear of showing up late? How can you offer solutions when every time you try to raise a red flag you're excluded from the conversation?

Eventually, as we saw in Chapter 8, Sunil was able to be vulnerable with Chris and share the reality of his situation. But before that breakthrough moment, team members didn't practice vulnerability; they practiced self-preservation. For many team members, this meant playing the blame game. Management in HR blamed their teams for missing their quotas. The HR teams blamed all the tardy employees for distracting them. The tardy employees blamed the weather, their dog, or anything else for deflecting attention from the fact that they were miserable at their job—but also terrified of losing it.

Such was the state of Softway in 2015. Unforgiveness and mistrust were everywhere. The system we had built was fundamentally broken. Eventually, something had to give—and it did, in the form of our 2015 downturn.

Afterward, we finally began to understand that initiatives such as our biometric scanners didn't fail because we had a tech problem or hadn't built good processes around them. They failed because we had a *people* problem. You can have as many alignment meetings as you want. If the people in that room don't feel empowered to do their jobs, if they don't feel that they can trust each other or that you have their best interests in mind, you're still going to have issues. Even worse, no one will be invested in fixing them. They'll just hand off the problem to someone else and play the blame game when things don't work out. In such an environment, layering more processes on top of the dysfunction will only make it worse.

> People's problems aren't fixed through process and technology. They're fixed through culture, behavior, and team dynamics.

INSPECTING AND INTROSPECTING YOUR SYSTEMS

When confronted with a system that doesn't work as it should, we often look for ways to tweak, add to, or otherwise modify the system. Rarely do we ask whether the system itself is critically flawed. As you examine your own systems, ask:

- When you designed your processes or adopted new technologies, what outcomes did you envision? What outcomes did you actually produce?
- How might your processes and tech adoption be hindering your people—and therefore your organization—from fully thriving?
- How would your systems change if you designed them around the Six Pillars of Love? What kinds of attitudes, mindsets, and behaviors would those systems promote? How would your processes and tech adoption change?
- Finally, how can you integrate your values into the day-to-day realities of your business decisions?

DON'T GET TRAPPED

Since its beginning, Softway has been in the business of solving problems for other businesses. But it wasn't until we began to introspect and understand our own problems that we were able to fully deliver on that promise to our customers. To do that, we had to learn to build our systems around our people, not on processes or technology.

Slowly, things began to change. Once our team members felt psychologically safe that they could speak and give feedback freely, we began to innovate in ways we never had before. Further, these changes could be felt throughout the organization—from our sales team to our project managers, from our creatives to our technologists. Because our systems were all designed to reflect our investment in our teams, our teams invested in us.

It took time to turn the ship, but eventually the results spoke for themselves. In 2015, we had low average contract values, little repeat business, and process issues that put our project managers and fulfillment team into perpetual firefighting mode. By 2019, our average client value had quintupled, we were consistently attracting repeat business, and we had repositioned ourselves to partner with clients and create lasting change rather than put out fires for them. The transformation was astonishing.

Again, this transformation wasn't about a process or a tech change—though those happened too. Instead, we looked at the dysfunction, unforgiveness, and mistrust inherent in our system and made a people change.

Many businesses like to look at processes as if they occurred in a vacuum, a set of gears in a machine. However, all processes are made by people. Most processes are performed by people. And yet somehow, whether we're designing or executing these processes, we often forget the fundamental humanity that drives them. This is why the Six Pillars are so important; they remind us of this fundamental humanity and make sure we never stray too far from it.

Softway's transformation wasn't about a process or new tech tool. It was about people being able to come together and collaborate in a safe space. It was about showing empathy for the customer's environment. When we had our pillars in place, we unlocked innovation and became a high-functioning business.

Love led to success.

Like many businesses, it was easy for us to fall into the process trap. But eventually, we were struggling to find our way through a labyrinth that none of us could keep track of or understand why it was built in the first place. All we knew was that this labyrinth had come to dominate the way we experienced our work, and it was making everyone miserable.

We didn't *want* to be miserable, of course. Even when we installed our biometric scanners, for instance, we had good intentions. We truly believed we were helping our team members do their jobs better. However, what we intended was not what happened—team members docked for legitimate leave, HR members behaving like truant officers, an angry CEO fuming over arrival data and accusing his entire organization of being lazy.

Not only was this "efficient" process highly inefficient in practice, but it also caused legitimate harm to the people it was supposed to help. When we docked their pay without warning, we made it harder for team members to provide for their families. When we forced HR to police the entire workforce, it prevented them from achieving their actual goals. When Mohammad focused solely on mistrust and unforgiveness, it prevented him from inspiring his teams and driving innovation within the company.

Whatever transformation you are trying to bring to your own organization, never forget that processes and technology merely reflect the decisions made by people. Do those people have the right mindset and behaviors? Are they supporting and empowering team members or putting them in a pressure cooker of mistrust? To drive the outcomes that will take your organization to the next level, you must start with people.

PUTTING PEOPLE FIRST

To learn more about how Softway found a balance between process and behaviors, visit LoveAsABusinessStrategy.com.

CHAPTER 14

LOVIN' THOSE BUSINESS OUTCOMES

Throughout this book, we've alluded to the big downturn that led to our darkest day, when we laid off a hundred employees in late 2015. Let's talk about how bad it actually was.

From late 2015 through 2016, Softway was on the verge of bankruptcy. With a negative 15 percent EBITDA or losses, we were hemorrhaging cash and staring down the reality of seven-figure losses. We owed everyone money—the banks, the credit card companies, and our landlords. Meanwhile, Mohammad had liquidated all his assets to keep the company afloat, even borrowing money from his family. While we had tried to be proactive with our layoffs, in reality it was already too little, too late. Whatever relief we got by reducing payroll wasn't nearly enough. The systemic issues created by our culture of fear were very nearly our undoing.

So when people ask us if going all-in on a culture of love *really* improves business outcomes, we point to ourselves as example Number 1.

Here, the numbers really do tell the story of just how remarkable our turnaround was. At the end of 2019, just three years after Softway almost went under, our company was growing and profitable. We not only increased our EBITDA to 28 percent (that's a 43 percent net difference!), but we also tripled our revenue. We had paid off all our debt. No matter which of the following metrics you want to look at, each can be traced back to our success at adopting a culture of love:

From 2016 to 2019, we saw the following improvements in our business outcomes:

Revenue: Increased by 300 percent

EBITDA or profit: Increased by 43 percent bringing it to a positive 28 percent

Average project size: Increased by 750 percent, putting our contracts into six and seven figures

Average account size: Increased by 985 percent

Client retention rate: Grew from 60 to 90 percent

Revenue per employee: Increased by 269 percent

Attrition: In 2016, our attrition rate was over 30 percent. In 2019, our combined average attrition for India and the United States was sitting at just 12 percent. (For comparison, the technology industry in the United States averages 13 percent attrition, while in India it averages 28 percent. We had lower attrition than our peers in both countries.)

Glassdoor rating: Our team members are not only staying longer, but they are also happier. In 2016, our Glassdoor rating stood at an unremarkable 2.9. As of this writing, that rating is well above 4.0. We are proud to say our team members feel the culture of love and belonging.

As remarkable as all of that is, here's what the numbers don't say. For years before our downturn, Softway had looked like a success. And on paper, we were. But our unforgiveness, misbehaviors, and structural greed caught up to us. The issues became so systemic that we stopped making money.

Through our transformation, we learned a valuable lesson—one that applies to any business of any size and in any industry. If you're a leader and all you're doing is looking at your bottom line and watching your account grow quarter over quarter, you might think you're okay. But what problems are sitting just below the surface? What are the numbers hiding that you're not bothering to look for? We didn't even think about addressing our problems until it was almost too late. Like many companies, we looked at our issues, shrugged, and said, "That's just the way we're built." But eventually, our denial led to real pain.

Your story doesn't have to be our story. You have the opportunity to change now—before your own systemic misbehaviors catch up to you.

Ultimately, a culture of love isn't even about change, but about opportunity. What opportunities could you embrace if your culture changed for the better? What could your people do if they were empowered and supported? When you ignore your people, when you exclude and marginalize, you're leaving money on the table. But when you care about your people and commit to building a culture of love around them, your business outcomes will improve in almost every way.

To be clear, those outcomes may look different than the ones you learned about in business school—and that's a good thing. We can talk all day about the ways in which our traditional metrics have improved since adopting a culture of love. However, if anything, those are lagging indicators of our commitment to our people. After all, revenue bumps are nice, but so is the money saved in improved employee retention. In this chapter, we're going to show the outcomes that we're most focused on in our own organization, and why a people-centric approach is the best way to get the results that really matter.

WHAT DRIVES OUTCOMES? PEOPLE

Softway works in technology. We like data. A lot.

Data gives you the background you need to be confident about your decisions and the direction in which you're moving. That said, data alone shouldn't drive your decision-making, because the numbers alone will never tell you the whole story. After all, behind every number, behind every metric, are the people who create them.

People are the biggest driver of business sustainability. Period. Human beings ladder up to revenue faster than any other investment your organization could make. Think of it this way: all of your outcomes are the work of people, the result of their behaviors. If you want to move the needle, then go back to your people, go back to the behaviors you want to see, and consider how you can invest in your people to create the outcomes you're looking for.

If you want your team to feel sharp and ready to work on an international trip, then invest in your team by bumping them all to business class on their flight over. If you want to create high-performing teams, then teach your teams how to build trusting relationships. If you want repeat business, serve your teams so they can serve your customer. Penny-pinching when it comes to your people is antithetical to a culture of love. In almost every case, the investment will be worth it because it galvanizes one important truth: your people feel taken care of.

In the following sections, we'll examine how a people-focused approach can help drive the outcomes that will position your organization for long-term success.

WINNING THE TALENT WAR WITH LOVE

There has always been and always will be a war for talent. Every company is looking for the best and brightest. When that talent knows that you are invested in creating and promoting a culture of love, that gives you a competitive edge. More and more talented individuals will want to work for you—and as a result, you'll have a much easier time identifying, recruiting, and promoting both leaders and role players within your organization.

How do we measure our success in winning the talent wars? For us, the key measurement is simple: do Softway team members like coming to work, and how would we know if they do? One key indicator your team members like coming to work is through referrals. Our team members constantly refer good candidates. In fact, we can often fill positions on referrals alone—without ever having to put up a job posting!

This is a great position to be in—and a far cry from a few years earlier, when we'd take out job ads and spend endless days and lots of dollars headhunting on LinkedIn, with all too little (if any) success. Many other companies we know of rely heavily on bonuses and incentives to bring in referrals. Nowadays, recruiting for us is often as simple as telling our team what positions are open and what we're looking for. Before we know it, six team members have suggested friends who are eager for the opportunity to come work at Softway.

Of course, we don't rely entirely on referrals. We still recruit externally too, though it's a lot easier these days. Before, potential candidates often wouldn't even return our calls or messages. These days, prospective candidates are intrigued by our culture of love and happy to respond. From there, it's just a matter of connecting with the recruits on a half-hour call and telling them what we're all about.

Here again, our focus on people makes a difference, with recruits often going out of their way to schedule an interview and meet us in person. As a result, we've gained access to much better talent, often attracting candidates who have turned down well-known organizations and much larger salaries to work at Softway. For a company like us, a mid-market challenger who has nowhere near the name recognition of the bigger fish like Google, our culture of love has given us a huge leg up when it comes to hiring. The talent we are able to attract reinvigorates the company.

How do we know that the top talent is choosing us over the

big fish? We ask them. Many of our candidates make no secret that they're also being pursued by larger players in the tech world. When they choose us, often they say that their decision came down to the recruiting experience they had and what they saw of our culture. Some went to Glassdoor to read our reviews and saw for themselves how we've improved in recent years.

RETAINING THE RIGHT PEOPLE

Once you've attracted good people, you need to retain them. After all, when a valued team member walks out the door, they take both their talent and their deep knowledge of your organization with them.

The talent you can replace. The knowledge, however, is a little trickier. According to some estimates, up to 60 percent of a person's role is undocumented—even in an organization that's great at documenting. In order to be successful, the next team member to inhabit the role needs to develop all of that knowledge from scratch. They'll get there eventually, but in the meantime, your organization pays the price in time and opportunity costs.

This challenge is only compounded the longer a person is with your company—the longer their tenure, the deeper knowledge they've accumulated, and the harder it is for their replacement to replicate the same knowledge and skillset. This is a lot to ask of any new recruit, and you're most likely going to have to pay for it—not only in terms of the lost time and opportunity cost, but also in the salary bump your new recruit is likely to command.

Many of these costs don't appear as an entry in the balance

sheet. They're hidden within so many other entries that leaders often don't see them. But the impact is real, and expensive. Every time you stop a high-performing person from walking out the door, you're keeping a pile of cash in the company's coffers.

"I'M NOT GOING ANYWHERE."

As a Black man, Chris has worked in many companies where the opportunities he had either were limited or required him to become someone he was not to get ahead. At Softway, Chris is empowered to be exactly who he is. He can make his mark on the world without worrying about the political games he would have to play elsewhere.

Like many of our other team members, Chris has thrived in this environment. And, also like many of our other team members, Chris is often approached by other companies attempting to poach him.

Every time Chris receives an offer or a message from another organization, the first thing he does is forward it along to Mohammad, along with a single sentence: "I'm not going anywhere."

Mohammad loves getting those emails.

Softway's reduced attrition rate isn't just good for business outcomes. It's also a great source of pride. When leaders and team members like Chris choose to stay—even in the face of temptation—it reinforces that our commitment to a culture of love is working. Softway team members aren't just here for a job, but to help build something bigger than themselves, a culture where everyone is valued and included regardless of background.

SAYING GOODBYE TO THE WRONG PEOPLE

While losing the right person is very costly, so is keeping the wrong person. Even in a culture of love (we would argue *especially* in a culture of love), you have to know when to let team members go.

In many organizations, people who are not contributing, not

resilient, and not behaving correctly often feel safe enough to ignore company policy. They are the ones who stay because they know that finding a job elsewhere would be difficult. In many organizations, these misbehaviors are tolerated at best and are unnoticed at worst. Meanwhile, each misbehavior poisons the culture a little more, alienating and driving away the best, most productive team members. Eventually the good people get tired of being hurt, and they leave to do their best work for someone else. At Softway, we've lost several rock stars we still miss, and we regret not stepping in to change the culture surrounding those star performers early and decisively.

At the same time, we have also struggled with a series of problematic leaders. Not everyone was on board with our shift to a culture of love. They rejected the chance to become servant leaders. They rejected our focus on people and our emphasis on growth, inclusion, and development. They did not see themselves clearly, they rejected feedback, and they rejected invitations to work on their behavior.

The differences between those leaders' teams and the teams of leaders who *had* embraced our culture of love were massive. In the loveless teams, team members were passive and micromanaged. Their leaders dictated exactly what to do, and as a result they adopted a passive mindset to disengage from their work and avoid accountability in a difficult environment. They were expected to stay at work till five on the dot every day, even if they were finished at four and had no more meaningful work left to do.

With no agency and no respect, their work suffered—often leaving us to play cleanup with angry clients. Moreover, our high-performing teams and team members began to take notice. Why was it okay for certain team leaders to skirt expectations and take advantage of our culture when everyone else was expected to uphold a higher standard? As more team members looked to senior leadership to see what we would do about the problem, we immediately saw that we had to find a solution. Approaching the problem from a growth mindset, first we tried to work with these problematic leaders. However, it became apparent that change wasn't possible; we accepted the fact that sometimes loving the entire team requires doing the right thing to support the whole team. Sometimes, that means letting people go who were not a good culture fit.

Fortunately, these problematic leaders were the exception, not the rule. Elsewhere, the teams whose leaders had embraced servant leadership excelled. Team members were able to work autonomously and produce innovative, creative solutions that our customers loved. These early results were proof positive that we were onto something with our new direction as a company. At the same time, because we hadn't shifted uniformly across the organization, we were delivering inconsistent results at best. During this period, it was like a tale of two companies. Unfortunately, we were slow to recognize the problem, identify the toxic leaders, and make their exits a priority—and it cost us. In the time we spent deciding, the leaders inflicted a lot of damage.

At Softway, love means we want everyone to be successful. We want to see the best for people, and we want them to grow. We are very tolerant of people who have problems with the executive leadership team. However, the moment a team member starts hurting others who are not their direct reports or part of the executive leadership team, we become far less tolerant. Such behavior is fundamentally antithetical to a culture of love. If that person is unwilling to change, then the only other choice is to exit them before they drive away the other team members we trust and value.

Having tough conversations is hard, but we cannot say that we love you and not tell you the truth. If you're not willing to follow the values that we live by, then you can't stay.

That being said, all people deserve to be treated with dignity and respect. We never want to go back to the dehumanizing way we laid off our employees in 2015. We let people go humanely. We give them a chance, and we show them what's required so that staying or going becomes their choice.

> We cannot love you so much that we allow you to harm others.
>
> We cannot allow people to take from the culture of love but not give back.
>
> We cannot allow people to abuse love.

PROJECT MANAGERS, FUTURE LEADERS

At Softway, we have found that project management is a tricky role to hire for. Relying on PMP certification didn't work; our projects and our clients are too varied. A single project manager might have to deal with moving parts from creative to technology, strategy to user experience, and everything in between.

At one point hiring PMs became like rolling the dice. We didn't know who would succeed and who would fail. Every project had its own challenges. There were too many surprises and pivots required to predict success in hiring.

As we grew as a people-focused organization, we became better at identifying the characteristics we desired in the PM role, and how to find the candidates who embodied them. In short, we wanted mini-CEOs, creative, autonomous thinkers who could treat each project as if it was their own little individual business. The best PMs ensure that their team innovates and delivers quality work. They understand every aspect of business and keep the project profitable. They negotiate and facilitate work between different members of different teams both within Softway and within the client organization on time—all while keeping everyone happy.

PMs, then, are the embodiment of servant leadership. They schedule meetings, order food, remove roadblocks, and otherwise grease the wheels of success. More than anything, they are resilient, adaptive, and able to work outside of the box. By prioritizing these traits in our hires—and then by trusting and empowering them from Day 1—we have not only solidified the role, but we have become far better at executing as a company.

As an added bonus, we have been able to incubate waves and waves of diverse, impactful leaders within our company. Our PMs regularly grow into other leadership positions. And because the role draws talent from a variety of backgrounds, it has also made our organizational leadership more diverse as a result—especially in terms of gender parity.

When you change the way you hire and provide opportunities for training and working on challenging projects, you change the skillsets in your organization. You enable people to grow, learn, fail, and take risks. When they do those things consistently, they'll earn promotions faster.

As you're hiring, look carefully at people from different backgrounds. Look beyond your backyard too. Our best PMs come from all over the globe. Pay particular attention to people who have service experience. Those people will be poised to adapt and eventually become servant leaders.

Finally, put your people in situations where they can be challenged and take risks, and entrust them with responsibility—and give them an environment where they can succeed. People tend to grow beyond the role they're given when you allow them to do it. When someone is capable of thinking broadly and finding solutions for the business and the customers, that person is ready to lead, regardless of the time they've spent in their role. So don't be surprised if you're promoting them within two years. Our best PMs make it to leadership extremely quickly.

BUSINESS SUSTAINABILITY

Companies often focus on the short term. Focused only on shareholder returns, they think only about the revenue they can bring in for the next quarter. But product cycles are quick. What you make today could be obsolete in a year. Further, short-term thinking tends to commodify your greatest resource: your people. If you're willing to put revenue ahead of your people so you can profit today, then why would you be expected to do anything different tomorrow?

If you build the right kind of organization, with the right people displaying the right attitudes and right behaviors, they will find the new products that need to be created. They will adjust to the new market conditions. They will stay ahead of the curve and embrace new ideas. They will create long-term possibilities without sacrificing short-term revenue.

Look at Blockbuster. A long time ago, in a galaxy far, far away, people would actually drive to stores like Blockbuster to rent DVDs of popular movies. They saw a business opportunity with streaming content long before Netflix—in fact, they even had an opportunity to purchase Netflix when the company was still in its infancy—but they never acted on these insights. They saw the idea of streaming content as a threat to their existing business model—specifically, to their huge profits on late fees and their in-store sales. Suffice it to say, their inaction bankrupted the organization. By the time they debuted their streaming service, Netflix already dominated the market. Blockbuster could not compete. Now, as of this writing, only one lone Blockbuster store remains, while Netflix is a flourishing international brand with hundreds of millions of customers.

One of the most important roles culture can play is in making the business sustainable. The old way is costly, rigid, and slow. A culture of love is resilient, adaptable, and innovative. It propels profit and long-term business outcomes.

THE IMPORTANCE OF RESILIENCE

Calamity and catastrophe come to every business in time. No one knows the future. There is no crystal ball. But you can be certain you will go through hard times. How your people respond when disaster strikes has everything to do with the culture you have built. That's why resilience is so important. If you build a team and an environment that can respond quickly to change, you'll survive the worst anyone can throw at you.

As we write this, we're seeing organizations fall to the economic uncertainty created by the COVID-19 crisis, while others thrive. Perhaps no industry has been harder hit than the airline industry. United Airlines, American Airlines, and Delta all furloughed thousands of employees—eventually laying many of those employees off. Southwest Airlines, however, was able to remain relatively successful.

So what did Southwest do differently? They doubled down on their strengths—servant leadership and love. No one was furloughed or laid off as a result of COVID. Instead, the organization temporarily reduced employee salaries so that everyone could keep their jobs. Knowing that this was a big ask, however, their CEO took the lead, announcing that he would take no salary whatsoever in 2020 and 2021.

Instead of making big, drastic choices that would be difficult to reverse, Southwest took smart operational steps. Moreover, because Southwest's model never depended on first-class or business-class offerings, they are poised to recover more quickly when the economy slowly lurches back to life. It's not easy keeping your cool under pressure like that—especially when that pressure is an era-defining pandemic. However, the organization's strong focus on love and servant leadership has produced a resilient culture that is more than capable of rolling with the punches.

As the late CEO of Oracle, Mark Hurd, once said, "Any idiot can cut costs. That's easy. The true measure of a leader is whether you can find revenue." When the COVID-19 pandemic hit us, we took these words to heart. Like an organization facing uncertain times, we were certainly interested in finding cost savings where we could. But, like Southwest, we weren't going to cut our people to do it. We'd seen that movie before, and we knew that wouldn't get us through the crisis—but resilience would.

Like many organizations, the first challenge we faced was having to rethink not only how teams worked, but also how they connected remotely. While our team members in America generally had internet access and could work from home, many of our team members in India did not have that luxury. When the pandemic hit, many of those team members returned to their hometowns to shelter in place. In these rural areas, internet connectivity was spotty at best. Through trial and error—and a lot of patience—we found a way to make it work.

As if that wasn't challenging enough, the pandemic also upended our entire business model. As a Houston-based organization, a large percentage of our clientele comes from the oil and gas industry—an industry that was already in the midst of a downturn before the pandemic. When the pandemic hit, it was like a double-whammy. Not only did we have to deal with the economic uncertainty of an international health crisis, but we also had to rethink not only how we served our clients, but also who our clients were. In order to survive, we realized that we would have to transition our business from a service-based model to a product-based model—and we'd have to do it from scratch.

Over the next several months, it was all hands on deck. Team members rose to the challenge, putting in extra hours, learning new skills, and supporting each other in service of the organization's shared goal. These efforts represented a huge sacrifice in time and energy, and yet our teams embraced the challenge with confidence and poise. As a result, we lived to fight another day.

Without resilience, that pivot never would have happened. But it wasn't the work that we put in during the pandemic that got us through—it was the work put in day in and day out for years beforehand. Resilience can't be bought off a shelf. It must be incubated and grown over time. From the very first moment we pivoted to a culture of love, we were positioning our company to weather the unprecedented storm that was 2020.

UNLOCK INNOVATION

Innovation is the ability to create new processes, products, technologies, policies, and tools—anything that gets the organization to a new level. Innovation creates new ways of coming together, of resilience, and of rising to the market's needs. You can only achieve innovation when people are comfortable speaking up and taking risks. It requires leadership to make space for others' ideas to shine.

Many companies turned the COVID crisis into innovation and opportunity. A car manufacturer transformed an assembly line to make ventilators within days. That didn't happen by accident. The change was made by people working together in a culture open to innovation, open to change. It required dismantling the old way to make room for the new.

When you are willing to abandon the old ways of working, you are ready for innovation. When you are committed to reaching the outcome by any path, when you are certain that you're serving the business, the people, and the customers in the marketplace, when you are open to ideas, you will find a way. You need a culture that supports and encourages these practices.

The culture of love naturally leads to these sorts of outcomes for your business. When you have a culture of love, you can build high-performing teams that practice inclusion, autonomy, empowerment, and all the rest. When you do so, you're creating an environment where people adapt, change, and are resilient. You're creating space for little moments of innovation that build toward something you couldn't have imagined before.

In a crisis, some companies create innovation. Some step up to market leadership. Southwest and others are poised to do just that in the aftermath of COVID-19.

CREATE BELONGING

Belonging can be difficult for leaders to grasp, because you can't see it as data on a dashboard. Moreover, while it's a popular word, no one is ever quite sure what it means.

Here's what it means to us. In early 2020, a large portion of our company took temporary pay cuts to get us through the economic downturn that resulted from the onset of the COVID-19 pandemic. Some on our executive leadership team even took cuts as high as 30 percent. Maggie was among the people who took the pay cut. Later on, once our business had stabilized, she told us she could have left and made more money elsewhere, but she didn't want to. In the five jobs she'd had up to that point in her career, she said she had never felt so respected and loved as she did in her job at Softway. This feeling extends both ways, which is why we asked her to write the book's foreword to honor the sacrifice and commitment that Maggie and so many other team members made.

Put simply, Maggie is part of our family. She *belongs*. Now that she's part of our family, she's forever a part of our family. Now that Softway is part of her identity, she will do whatever she can to fight for it, to protect it, and to defend it—even if that means sacrificing some of her own salary.

Of course, belonging to a family isn't all about sacrifice. It's also about feeling free to explore, to emote, and to be connected—the comfort of knowing that everyone has your back and that everyone's success is interconnected. Even if Maggie leaves the team, she will still hold onto these feelings (we hope), because she is a forever member.

This feeling of belonging is rare in many modern businesses, especially among younger generations and diverse talent. It's not that team members like Maggie don't want to belong to something that is bigger than themselves. It's that they've never worked for an organization that has invited them to do so. Regardless of generation, if you can unlock a feeling of belonging—this feeling of family—in your team members, you will be rewarded not only with higher retention, but with committed, dedicated team members.

This leads us to the ultimate outcome of belonging. When team members feel as if they belong to an organization, it also amplifies our sense of belonging as leaders. In turn, we are inspired to double down on what makes our culture strong—further boosting that sense of passion and purpose within the organization and triggering what we call a *legacy of belonging*.

When new team members come into the fold at Softway, they are inspired by all the love, passion, and dedication around them—accelerating their own buy-in and participation in the culture. As leaders, we're amazed at how welcome new team members are made to feel. We're amazed at how quickly they buy into the culture around them. And we're amazed at how far we've come as an organization to get here. For those of us who were around for Softway's darkest day, this is a special feeling indeed.

HOW BAD DO YOU WANT IT?

In 2019, we initiated a round of customer interviews to build empathy and to receive feedback. They told us we were not the cheapest, but we did good work, and they had a good time working with us. Every customer agreed that working with our team meant spending time with good humans.

So many companies try to be a market leader by engaging in a race to the bottom for the cheapest product. They don't care about quality, and they don't care about the people along the way. You're leaving money on the table when you do that. Worse, you are creating an image of your organization that will permeate the market. Customers know if your team is miserable. They know whether they're being taken care of properly or whether people are checking the boxes.

We've worked with many consultants from large firms. When we go out for social events, they tell us they wish they had what we have. For the most part they're hard-working people, but they aren't supported by their companies. They can't answer questions without getting guidance from a senior partner. The client knows that this is just how it's done, and feels the lack. Intimacy and empathy are lost in translation. Trust is lost because the leaders didn't set the consultants up for success, creating a burdensome chain of command that squashes opportunities to pivot in real time to customer needs.

As we'll share in the next chapter, when you build a business around people, on the other hand, customers will feel it. They will be drawn to you. We've had great opportunities come to Softway simply because people like working with us. They're drawn to our team.

Ultimately, that's what you get when you have a culture of love: people just want to be around you. But again, this isn't easy. Just as we found with some of our leaders, some people need more convincing—while others want nothing to do with it. That's why, in our last chapter, we're going to take a good, long look at what it takes to bring (and manage) lasting change within your organization.

CHAPTER 15

WAITING ON THE WORLD TO CHANGE?

Up to this point, we've talked a lot about how your mindsets, attitudes, and communication impact others. Here, in this last chapter, we're going to talk about how to make sweeping change real and tangible for others—something that takes diligent, consistent, and disciplined work.

Our own attempts to adopt Agile business processes are a good example of what to do—and more importantly, what not to do—to bring about organizational change. The first time we tried to go Agile was back in 2010. It failed. But by 2020—our third attempt—we finally succeeded. Why? Because this time, we focused on culture first, and that taught us some valuable lessons about how to communicate in a way that drives real change.

Our first attempt came in the dark times, pre-2015, back when our approach to everything was based on the traditional command-and-control model: our leaders would dictate the Agile processes they wanted to see, and then humiliate their team members when they messed up. Clearly, such behavior would never fly in a culture of love—but the worst part was that our leaders weren't adopting these Agile principles themselves. This created a "do as I say, not as I do" approach to Agile, one that quickly fizzled out when leaders lost interest and moved on.

The result was a complete and utter failure to adapt in any way. At the time, we were surprised to see our Agile initiative crash and burn. Now, we're a little older and a little wiser. At best, command-and-control is an outdated, marginally effective leadership style. In our case, all it was good for was alienating our team members and exposing our own hypocrisy.

The second time we tried to go Agile, we thought for sure the effort would stick. After all, by this time we had fully embraced the principles of love as a business strategy, and we had learned a thing or two about getting our team members to buy into big changes. This time, we would lead with education, winning over our teams' hearts and minds by carefully explaining what Agile was, why it worked so well, and why the transition was so important to our company.

But we forgot one thing: failure leaves a bitter taste—one that lingers for a long, long time. The team members who were around during the first go-round saw what a train wreck that attempt had been, and they weren't interested in trying again. We had the right idea of wanting to win over the hearts and minds of our team members, but we hadn't considered that the memory of our previous attempt would cast such a long shadow.

We also made another mistake during this second go-round:

we tried to adopt Agile across every team within the organization all at once without accounting for how these processes would translate to different departments. Our large creative team, for instance, didn't think Agile applied to them at all. How could a software development process possibly help them be more productive in their creative work?

We were certain that Agile could help our creatives quite a bit. However, convincing them proved difficult. Try as we might, we found very few resources or examples for how to implement Agile for their particular brand of creative work. They had questions, and we couldn't answer those questions in a clear, intuitive way. Fear stacked on top of fear, and the effort to bring Agile to Softway fizzled out once again.

In 2020, right in the middle of the COVID-19 pandemic, we decided to try again. And as it turned out, pivoting in the middle of a crisis turned out to be just the boost we needed. This time, our backs were against the wall; it was either pivot or die. With the stakes significantly higher this time around—and since we had to change anyway—we were able to get our teams on board across the company and make the changes stick.

Increasing our chances of success, we also added another crucial element to the process. Before making our pivot, we developed our operating principles document. These operating principles are rooted in Agile, but they are framed in a way that anybody can understand and apply. By focusing on these principles first and the processes second, our team members gained a deeper understanding of what we were trying to do. They understood not only the mechanics of Agile, but also the mindsets that drove it.

Once we had defined our principles, we looked for every opportunity we could to reinforce them. One of our favorite ways was through a series of short videos. Using humor to drive engagement, each video led with a principle and then offered examples of how the old Softway would approach a situation, followed by the Agile way, making it as easy as possible for team members to understand what behaviors would change. Further, we aligned leadership, making a conscious effort not only to reinforce our principles when we made decisions and planned projects but also in the language we used to give feedback.

Little by little, the ideas became practical and accessible. Team members couldn't escape them; they were everywhere at Softway. No matter what role they had, team members were able to find how they fit into the new operating rhythms our organization was adopting.

At long last, the change worked—thanks in part to necessity, in part to our improved ability to communicate what we wanted, and in part to the fact that our culture of love had matured over the last couple of years.

Ultimately, we see that culture of love as the difference-maker, the secret sauce that has given us an advantage over other Agile organizations. These days, we are able to easily move people from one stable team to another, if the work calls for it. You could be on one team for several sprints, and then be on another for the next several. Because every team operates under the same principles and the same culture of love, you can get up to speed and begin contributing immediately.

In a culture of love, you know what is required of you. You know you'll be included. You know you'll receive feedback and be asked to give feedback in return. You know that you'll be expected to approach your work in a certain way, no matter who you're working with.

Before our transformation, this wasn't the case—our culture was the Wild West, and you had to learn to make your own way (usually with a few arrows in your back for the effort). When every team had its own culture, leadership style, and way of working—switching teams was a major undertaking. Team members had to sit back and observe for extended periods of time before they could effectively contribute. Our operating principles translated our values into the day-to-day tactics of an Agile system. Sure, we had some bumps along the way, but because trust and feedback are inherent to a culture of love, we were able to work through them.

If you want to transition to a culture of love, or make any other big, sweeping transformation, you'll have to create real, lasting, meaningful change within yourself and your organization. But change is hard. Organizations routinely fail to change—despite our best efforts, we did twice.

Fortunately, change is possible. In this chapter, we'll discuss how to find your own personal case for change and help others do the same. We'll also discuss communication tools that can help you connect with your people, win them over, and make change stick.

But first let's consider the question: why is change so hard?

WHY CHANGE FAILS

Companies are under more pressure than ever to keep up in

a highly competitive marketplace—and they're prepared to invest heavily in their ability to do so. They want all the benefits of a big sweeping change like Agile, but when it comes time to implement, something gets lost in translation, and their efforts fizzle out (just as they did the first two times with us).

As it turns out, everyone wants change, but no one wants *to* change.

This isn't just idle chatter. Almost 84 percent of digital and organizational transformations fail.[9] We'd argue that most of them fail because of people. As we said in Chapter 13, change doesn't come through new processes or a new technology stack. Change comes through people and the decisions they make. If leaders are making decisions out of a lack of trust or a lack of empathy for their team members, just as Mohammad did when he implemented the biometric scanner system, that decision is going to fail.

Here's how the process usually goes down. Leadership decides they need to change, then they decide how they want to change. They know they need to convince their teams of this new initiative, but they try to do it by stating the business case for that change. Maybe the market conditions are changing. Maybe they need to double their revenue. Maybe they want to capture the marketplace. Maybe they want to become the number one manufacturer and supplier of Widget X in the world.

---

9   Phil Lewis. "Where Businesses Go Wrong with Digital Transformation." *Forbes*. July 31, 2019. https://www.forbes.com/sites/phillewis1/2019/07/31/where-businesses-go-wrong-with-digital-transformation/?sh=31fd8cf670bb

This might work for shareholders, but it's not very compelling to other stakeholders. The communication is heavy on corporate jargon and benefits to shareholders, but light on the things that actually matter to your average team member. Unless your team member can expect to double their paycheck when the company doubles its revenue, they have little reason to care. That's where the breakdown occurs. Without that reason to care, that change is nothing more than an arbitrary corporate goalpost. Team members have little reason to make the big and difficult switch to a new set of processes and behaviors.

Further compounding the issue is that leadership often treats change as something the rest of the organization needs to do, but that they don't have to do themselves. In recent years, many leaders have made this mistake with Agile. They hear that Agile is the way to go, so they invest in coaching, training, and change management for the entire organization—and then they sit back and wait. They're surprised when the organization can't change, and they're frustrated when the results don't come—blind to the fact that they themselves need to be the first adopters of Agile in order for it to be successful.

We know this because we lived it. The first time Softway tried to go Agile, Mohammad was all about command-and-control and corporate jargon. He was met with huge resistance. In contrast, when Mohammad was able to translate meaning to individuals and connect what mattered to them with the larger business case, the company saw better momentum, better buy-in, and better commitment—which ultimately led to actual, sustainable change.

To be clear, we aren't naive. We know that love alone will not enact change (which was the mistake we made the second time around). You can have the best idea and the best strategy in the world, but without a good change strategy and change hygiene, you will face resistance. To see successful change inside an organization, you will have to get every individual in the organization committed. In order to do that, change must feel personal. Leaders must model what's needed. Every change should be approached through the lens of empathy. Each and every team member must be able to connect with it and why they benefit, in plain language.

So where do you start? The first step in communicating change is explaining *why* you are changing, and how the change fits within the larger vision of the company.

START WITH VISION AND VALUES

Pop quiz time. Right now, off the top of your head, do you know what your company's vision and values are?

If you're not sure, don't worry—you're far from alone. In fact, if you asked the average team member what our vision and values were before 2015, they probably wouldn't have been able to tell you either. The reason why? Our vision wasn't memorable. See for yourself:

> **Softway pre-2016:** To be the best digital agency and the best technology company in the world.

For lack of a better word, our old vision was fluffy. It wasn't specific to our company at all—hundreds of other companies have set similar visions. Further, it wasn't directional. It didn't tell us where to go, or specifically how to succeed. The result was a wholly uninspiring bit of corporate-speak. Now, let's compare that old vision to our new one:

Softway post-2016: To bring back humanity to the workplace.

Once we pivoted to a culture of love, we knew that it was time to reset our vision and set Softway's eyes on a new path. This wasn't a strategic PR move. Our goal wasn't to revamp our public-facing statement and then build a big campaign around our new vision. We saw this as a reckoning, a chance to ditch the corporate-speak, ask ourselves what we truly believed in, and use that as our foundation to rebuild the company. We wanted a vision that was specific, inspirational, and uniting. When team members heard our vision, we wanted them to connect with it, to see themselves in it, to be inspired and motivated to fight for that vision day in and day out. Without that personal connection, our culture of love would never be able to reach its full potential.

If your vision doesn't do that, then rework it. If the new vision doesn't do that, then rework it again—as many times as it takes to get it right.

That might sound like a lot of work, but it's worth it. Every company should have a vision, and everybody who works there should be able to see themselves in it. (If someone can't see themselves in a particular company's vision, that's fine; not everyone has to work for the same company.)

From there, it's important to define your values. Values can take on different forms in different organizations. For us, our values are defined in our Six Pillars of Love and in our operating principles. Through these documents, our team members receive clear guidance on how to translate our vision—to bring humanity back to the workplace—to tangible, consistent behaviors.

That's the key to good values. They must tie in clearly to your vision, they must be specific, and they must be actionable. Too often, organizations spend boatloads of money on consultants to define and adopt values that sound really good, but that are ultimately flat and meaningless. Values like "integrity," "excellence," and "fairness" might sound great on paper, but what do they mean? How do you put them into action?

To make sense, values must be wedded to behaviors. We recommend starting with behaviors that illuminate your values—such as our Six Pillars of Love. Then, just as you saw in Part 2, make sure to define these values with specific examples so your team understands what it looks like to apply those values in their day-to-day work. When you focus on behaviors, you ground the conversation and make it practical.

Vision and values have the potential to unite people behind change. They can become the mindsets that drive action. But if there is a misalignment between the values on paper and the actions in reality, that will feed mistrust and pushback. This is why strong, empathetic leadership around your vision and values is so important. Alignment around visions and values must start at the senior-most level. Leaders must model the values and the change they want to see through their own behavior. If you can do that successfully, then alignment around your vision and values will grow throughout your organization.

Of course, to begin the process of driving that change, you first need to understand what that change means to you.

MAKE A PERSONAL CASE FOR CHANGE

In 2020, the COVID-19 pandemic forced Softway to pivot from our approach as a service-based organization to a products and solutions model. Needless to say, that was a big pivot for an organization—which is why it was so important that we adopted an Agile framework that would allow us to make such a big pivot.

The business case for this shift was clear: the new products and services model would offer more opportunities to drive long-term, sustainable revenue at higher margins. Having more forecastability and stability would get us through the uncertain times.

Now, here's the thing. Every big change needs a corresponding business case. But even a good business case on its own is pretty abstract—it's not exactly the kind of inspiring statement to drive people's behaviors. So, when we set out to drive and champion this change, we each took some time to make a personal case for change as well. Here's what the four of us had to say:

> Frank is motivated by helping people feel less like imposters and more like team members. Frank wants to be part of creating a lasting legacy that will positively impact people, whether that's more financial security for people or a workplace where people feel a deep sense of belonging, unafraid to bring their full selves to work. Frank working toward this goal is rejuvenating. He can see the impact that he personally has on the lives around him, even if his name will never be attached to the work.

> Chris sees a changing world. The pandemic has made life fundamentally different, and people must adapt. For some people, the change is frightening, but for Chris, it's an open space with limitless opportunities. He has the ability to take stock of what works and what doesn't, what he likes and what he doesn't, where he is in his life and where he wants to go and to rewrite his future accordingly. To him, change means being able to literally rewrite his destiny. Softway's change becomes part of that.

> Jeff spends a lot of time connecting with old friends on social

media and seeing what they're up to. Too often, he hears stories of how businesses are treating their employees—and none of them are good. He's driven to help change this—even if it's one company or one team at a time. Softway's story and transformation are something that he fully experienced, and it transformed him as well. He knows that the same meaning and purpose can be found for others. Going through his own personal transformation has also made him a better husband, father, and friend—so he's driven to keep focusing and working on himself.

Mohammad has become increasingly invested in spending time with his family in recent years, but juggling his business and his home life has been intense. However, he knows that this intensity is not only unsustainable, but unhealthy for his family. Mohammad himself grew up in a household where his father worked long hours in a toxic workplace just to provide for his kids, and he doesn't want his kids growing up in the same kind of environment. Mohammad knows that many other families struggle with similar problems. If he can solve this problem for others by creating a more stable and predictable environment at Softway, then he can solve it for himself as well—affording him the much-needed opportunity to spend time with his children.

Now, here's the question: In leading your organization to a culture of love, what might your personal case for change look like? What motivates you? What drives you, beyond salary or revenue? How does your personal case connect with your business case?

Naturally, we can't tell you your own personal case for change. Only you will know your reasons, based on your experience, your life, and your goals and vision for yourself, your team, and your organization. However, we can offer some ideas and starting points, based on the responses from the participants in our Seneca Leaders workshops:

Leaving a legacy. Many senior leaders want to be remembered not just for their accomplishments, but for how well they treated other people. They're willing to change, to embrace new mindsets and behaviors, because they don't want to be remembered as someone whom people dreaded working with. They want people to come to their funeral.

Starting off strong. Many young leaders are often interested in starting off strong. They want to be everyone's best boss. They want to accomplish great things. They don't want to build up a set of bad behavior or habits that they'll have to spend the rest of their careers undoing.

More stability. Some people just want to come to work each day and be happier. They want to do the right thing and are willing to change whatever is necessary to make going to work something that they look forward to.

Some leaders said they often misbehaved with team members. They wanted to ask for forgiveness and make amends so that they could be the leaders that people look up to.

Individual contributors wanted to treat their team members better because they saw the impact of their behavior. Referencing our Six Pillars, they would say things like, "I want to be more empathetic because I realize that people at work also have lives at home." Or, "I want to make people feel included and give them a safe space to share when they're dealing with something." Rarely did the business case come up.

It's our hope that these examples have given you a few starting points. But whatever the case, before trying to bring change to your own organization, take some time to be clear on what this change means for you and your own goals. This personal case for change will allow you to remain on course, do the hard work, and lead by example day by day.

MAKE YOUR CASE

Still unsure how to write a really great case for change? We've got plenty of change strategy resources to walk you through it at LoveAsA BusinessStrategy.com.

COMMUNICATING CHANGE

Having your business case and your personal case for change is only half the battle. Now, you need to communicate that change—what it is, why you're doing it, and *how* you're doing it. After all, it doesn't matter what you say if no one will listen.

So, what does communicating change look like in a culture of love? First, it means considering the other person's perspective first. In other words, know your audience, and communicate to them human to human (always keeping the Platinum Rule in mind). That way, your communication will not only be more real, but also more memorable.

Next, work to make all your communications—no matter what form they come in—more relevant and engaging. From there, focus on the lesson you're hoping to teach. After all, as

Chris's sister likes to say, "You gotta give them broccoli with their brownies."

From there, go out of your way to connect people with what you're sending out. Use plain language, not corporate jargon. Communicate "to the last seat," to the person all the way on the front lines. Make the communication valuable to the end user, and they will respond. If your team members have to learn facts, such as compliance or strategy policies, and you have to have adherence, being forceful or dry will do no good. Find a way to put that broccoli into a brownie.

We've seen the power of this approach not only in our own communications, but in the campaigns we've helped produce for other organizations as well. For instance, we once created a campaign for one of our energy clients to bring levity to the world of cybersecurity through a series of comedic video tutorials. At first, we weren't sure if the client would go for the idea, since they're relatively risk-averse. After they agreed to let us test the waters with a short series of videos, we eagerly got to work.

Our premise was simple, yet compelling. Each short featured two characters, one a bad actor trying to launch a cyberattack against the company, and the other a clueless employee. In each episode, the employee inevitably let the bad actor in, and hilarity would ensue.

The concept was an instant hit. In fact, the first video quickly became the most-watched piece of content within the whole organization. The characters even became so popular in Europe that they began showing up on their campus billboards. We were glad this organization's team members liked our brownies, but the good news was that they were also enjoying the broccoli—which, of course, was the whole point of the campaign. Team members became more cautious about how they engaged on LinkedIn or Facebook, as well as more cautious about opening emails; team members regularly began checking in with cybersecurity before sending sensitive communications out, and got better about flagging suspicious emails.

Taking the light approach doesn't always work. For instance, you would never want to joke around in communications about upcoming layoffs or pay cuts. The point is, when you know your audience, you can find the appropriate amount of levity, vulnerability, and transparency for your situation. Here are some other things to keep in mind to help you strike that just-right balance.

MAKE FAILURE PART OF THE PROCESS

In 2010, Finland introduced the world to the International Day for Failure. Every year on October 13th, people are encouraged to share their failures. In the years since, leaders, politicians, and celebrities have all joined in on the fun, sharing failures both big and small with anyone who is interested.

We think this is a great idea.

If everyone is talking about failure, then it becomes obvious that it's a natural part of learning and growth. That's how the doctors and nurses learned to improve their performance in Amy Edmondson's landmark study, and that's how you and the other leaders can improve learning within your own organization. Leaders who are willing to share their mistakes show that it's okay to fail. As a result, team members become more willing to share and learn from their own failures, and the organization becomes more resilient.

Making failure part of the process is another way to humanize your communication and make your message more relatable to your team. After all, communication is hard. You *will* get things wrong. Ask for and receive feedback, and commit to learning from failure—both your own and those among your team—over time. And always remember: it's better to communicate, even imperfectly, than to get stuck in silence.

MAKE IT ABOUT PEOPLE

In one 7,000-person organization we worked with, people saw senior leaders as gods on Olympus, aloof and removed from the everyday world. They knew nothing about them as people. Was the VP married? Did he have kids? Where was he from? No one knew.

It was our job to change that. So, we created a campaign where we interviewed leaders for five to seven minutes apiece, and almost none of our questions had to do with work. Instead, we asked things like where they went to school, what their friends were like, who their family was, what their favorite TV shows were, and so on. Sometimes we ate ice cream with them on camera—other times we hosted push-up competitions.

After the videos were released, the difference was immediate. For instance, one of the leaders was a big fan of *Game of Thrones*. Once his team members knew that, they knew they had something to talk to him about when they bumped into him in the hallways. When you show people who you are behind the job title, you become more approachable—more human. As a result, you build a level of comfort and a relationship that wasn't there before.

This kind of vulnerable, human-interest focus may just feel like filler, but it is everything to the health of an organization—especially to an organization in the middle of a big transformation. If you close off and stay stuffy and stoic, you won't connect with anyone, and no one will connect with you. This doesn't do anyone any good. After all, many of us spend more time with our fellow team members than we do with our own friends and family. Do you *really* want to spend so much of your time with complete strangers? Nearly any message will be more engaging, more memorable—and more effective in making a case for change—when it's delivered by someone you know.

BE TRANSPARENT (TO A DEGREE)

Transparency is trendy. Everyone wants to know what's happening in real time. We like transparency too. In fact, we've argued for sharing important information with team members several times. People will make more responsible cost decisions if they can see the impact on the bottom line, for example.

That said, especially when it comes to communicating for change, it is possible to be too transparent.

Leaders are sometimes under great pressure to share information, but if they share too little information too soon, it doesn't help anyone. People won't respond well to uncertain or incomplete information. Instead of giving your teams clarity, you only get a barrage of questions that you can't answer.

Worse, if you share incomplete information too soon, you create opportunities for people to doubt the change. They feel as if you've failed to develop a coherent plan at an important moment. Then, in addition to finalizing all your plans, you'll also be stuck trying to mitigate chaos as your message travels through the grapevine.

Nature abhors a vacuum. In the face of incomplete information, people will make up their own answers to fill in the gaps. Back-channel conversations will lead to instability and fear. They'll create a distraction, disruption, and a lack of productivity. When the full truth arrives, even though you and your team were careful in your planning, many will still distrust it.

To sum up: it's essential for internal communication to build trust. Handled correctly, it is an extension of a culture of love. Using transparency responsibly is part of that. But sharing too much too soon is not an act of love—it's an act of sabotage.

So let's define responsible transparency. Responsible transparency recognizes that there are different degrees of information sharing. Let's say you're about to undergo a reorganization. Reorgs usually take several months of careful planning across divisions, and ultimately they affect everyone's job. Naturally, when people know a reorg is coming, they'll want to know what it means for them—even before you have the answers.

In such a situation, you can do two things. One, you can fudge it, and leave your team members with a growing sense of uncertainty and dread. Or two, you can be transparent about the fact that you're not ready to answer the question yet. In this case, you would explain that there will indeed be changes, but that you want to come back with a well-thought-out response that will answer all of their questions. But for right now, you're still in the process of gathering information.

By managing expectations, you show that you are being responsible and not approaching your reorg in a haphazard way. Releasing information too soon, before you can detail how it will affect individual people, is never good.

As the saying goes, *ask us how we know*. You know those first two attempts to switch to Agile that didn't quite pan out? Well, those misfires led to several hours of one-on-ones and team meetings to clean up the damage and reassure the many, many anxious team members throughout the organization.

So when should you be transparent right away, even when you might not know all the answers at the moment? Again, the COVID-19 pandemic serves as a good example. In such a situation, it would have been strange if we *didn't* speak up. Here, we were fully transparent: we were still processing the situation and how it impacted us, but we wanted to be available to answer any questions or how any economic downturn might affect the company. We also wanted to make ourselves available to any team member who wanted to discuss how the pandemic was impacting them personally.

In situations like this, the best policy is to quickly get in front of the situation. Everyone knows that it will take time to understand it. No one has a crystal ball. Speaking up then will earn more trust than staying silent.

Here is where your investment in your culture will pay off. A culture of love will promote resiliency, and the more resilient your culture is, the more your people can adapt with you. Communicating in a loving way without excess uncertainty is part of that.

LEADERSHIP AND COMMUNICATION

When you're a leader, receiving communication can sometimes feel as if you're getting a watermelon. It's green on the outside, so it looks good. But then, you open it up to find out it's red. The information is far from good—in fact the world is on fire!

Your team members may mean well, but they're often inclined to deliver news in a way they think their leaders want to hear it. As a result, finding the truth can be an exercise in disappointment and frustration.

To get accurate information, and to be able to understand what your people need to hear and how, it's important to build a network of people who will tell you the truth without sugarcoating—people who understand how your teams are doing, what they're experiencing, and what their needs are. That way, you can more effectively take the temperature of the room so that you can respond with empathy, and without losing track of your goal among the details.

Ask questions. Get feedback. Speak with your listeners in mind. However, do not allow analysis paralysis to stop you from getting at the truth.

BUILDING CHANGE NETWORKS

Every political movement requires a grassroots organization. A community must knock on doors, raise money, facilitate communications, and set up meetings with special interest groups to turn out the vote. Similarly, organizations depend on internal change networks to help drive any new initiative.

Change networks influence team members around them to behave differently, manage differently, and even be led differently. As we saw with our many attempts to go Agile, this is no easy task. After all, change requires people to be convinced, one by one, to become believers. As a leader, it's important to lead by example, to share your own personal case for change, and to lead communication efforts to help get everyone on the same page. However, you can't influence everyone by yourself. The true work of change begins when you have built a network of people within the company who are all committed to helping you champion the change.

When building your change network, you need change agents. Here are some traits to look for:

People who naturally have the gift of speaking truth to power.

Influencers who are good at convincing others to be uncomfortable and take smart risks.

Pioneers who are always looking for the best path forward.

Communicators who are good go-betweens for teams and leadership.

Team members with a finger on the pulse—who know how organizational messages are being received (and how you might want to adjust going forward).

Leaders need accurate information about how things are going on the ground. Change agents set up a positive feedback loop that not only helps the leader set the tone, but that also builds advocacy and buy-in and helps the organization become aligned. Once you have identified these change agents, your change networks will grow, and change will begin to take root organically.

With that said, this isn't a one-and-done effort. You don't build your change networks and then call them good. Change networks require maintenance—and you neglect their care at your own peril.

The big reason for this is natural, good old-fashioned human skepticism. Love is powerful and transformative. Unfortunately, not everyone is going to jump on the love horse with you and ride off into the sunset. You, your change agents, and your change networks will inevitably encounter skeptics. This has happened to us with every initiative both before our pivot to a culture of love and after, and it will happen to you too.

People see skeptics as disbelievers, barnacles, and enemies, people who will resist you no matter what you say. The truth, however, is different. A skeptic is someone who has not yet understood the value of what you're trying to do. They are naturally going to inquire, test, seek validation, and do research, and others are going to learn from their example. In other words, skeptics mobilize people—and that's a good thing! Your job is to be ready to earn their belief, and to speak about your personal reasons for change.

But here's the good news: your biggest skeptics also have the greatest potential to drive change within your organization.

This is why we put so much emphasis on your personal case for change at the beginning of the chapter.

Your reasons matter, because it is your behavior and your

influence that will ground the change. You will have to fully commit before anyone else will believe.

Lead with your new behavior and wait to be asked about it. Skeptics will listen to your personal story, if it feels authentic. Perhaps you can talk about wanting to leave a better legacy, or setting your team up for success. Whatever your story is, if you are acting in accordance with it, you will be listened to. You will have the opportunity then to explain why you want the change.

Have open conversations with skeptics. Get to the bottom of their concerns. If you're shepherding a change into the culture of love, talk about the terms you're using—like love, forgiveness, empathy, and trust—and share what they mean both to you and to the organization. Ask what the risks are in treating people better.

Then, walk them through the reality of what a better work-place could look like. Ask them to imagine how it could make their lives—and their teammates' lives—better. Then (and only then), explain the business case, discussing the improved outcomes of high-performing teams, more inno-vation, more revenue, lower turnover, and so on.

Make the case, one skeptic at a time. If you can convince and convert them, they will become your biggest advocates. Naturally, you will still need your change networks and your change agents to make change stick, but these one-on-one conversations can make powerful allies.

PROOF IN ACTION

In the business world, when we consider change, our minds almost immediately turn to metrics and data. We've talked elsewhere about how, although we value these tools as well, we also see them as part of a more holistic view of change. Far too often, organizations will attempt a change, look at a narrow band of data and metrics, and get frustrated when they see few indications of the change they were hoping to create.

If all you're looking for is quick results, then hire a consulting firm to retool your values and launch a PR campaign around them. Just don't expect whatever bump you get to last. However, if you're looking to create lasting change, then you must be willing to put in deep, sustained work for a long time before you see any measurable results at all.

Think back to the beginning of this book, all the way to Part 1, where we described our philosophy of love. There's a reason we modeled that philosophy like a building: foundation first, then supporting infrastructure, and then the finishing touches. While it's the first two parts that are the most important, it's the third part that everybody notices.

But make no mistake, if you put in the work, others *will* notice eventually.

We were nearly two years into our transformation before our customers noticed the difference in our culture. But when they did notice the change, they saw it everywhere. They saw it in how our teams performed. They saw it in the way we communicated both with them and with each other—always with kindness and respect. They saw the ideas we brought to the table. They saw it in Mohammad, in Softway's leaders, and in every single team they interacted with.

Perhaps most noticeably, they saw the difference it made in terms of the outcomes we created for them. Customers gave us more and more trust as a result of our behavior change. As a result, they spent more money—a lot more money—and we began to see a lot more repeat business.

As you can imagine, customers can be your biggest skeptics. Yet, in the end, they saw the transformation we had gone through; they saw the difference it made in how we approached our work, and they wanted it for themselves. So, they asked us to teach them how we did it. After a messy but successful pilot, the Seneca Leaders program was born (see Chapter 8).

These days, the Seneca Leaders program has helped us teach love as a business strategy to thousands of business leaders across the world. (We've even written a book about it!) But at the time, this was uncharted territory. We'd never consulted in that space—or even imagined it. We'd gone through our transformation to a culture of love purely out of need. But the results spoke for themselves, and we were happy to seize on this new (and unexpected) business opportunity.

Also, we didn't want to screw it up. For the next several weeks, everyone in the organization stepped up to make sure we not only proved the value of a culture of love, but also created something really special. It was tense—especially because not everybody on our clients' executive leadership team was on board. We challenged them and pushed hard. In fact, we even had members of their team write anonymous letters about the organization's leadership. Then, we asked the executive leadership team to read those letters aloud to each other.

That got us to the next step: a one-off workshop in South America. Afterward, the executive leadership team brought us back and asked his people on the ground whether they should continue to roll out this training. The participants literally cried when we asked them for feedback after the workshop, telling us how impactful and incredible the experience had been. They had enjoyed the experience so thoroughly—and received so much value from it—that they demanded it be rolled out for the entire company.

We didn't ask for this full-throated approval, but we were sure happy to get it.

After that day, even the skeptics were convinced. Soon, they had funded a multimillion-dollar program based solely on the impact it had had on that one group.

Nothing will convince a skeptic faster than consistent behavior change and consistent results. It takes time. However, when you convince them, they become your greatest ally.

How can you make your change personal to people? How can you show them results? How can you communicate in a way that is not only engaging, but also compelling? How can you sneak the broccoli into the brownie?

Change *is* possible, but your words and behaviors are what will convince people to change.

Ultimately, that is the best kind of proof—the proof in action.

CONCLUSION

NO MORE EXCUSES

Now that you've reached the end, we're going to make a prediction.

As you were reading this book, there was a little voice in your head reading along with you. With each new story you read, with each new concept you learned, that voice tried to convince you to quit before you even began:

"Sure, that worked for them, but that would never work in our company."

"I could never get leadership to commit to this."

"This is way more effort than I can handle right now."

Sound familiar? Whatever that voice said, it was speaking in the language of a fixed mindset. The question is, are you going to listen to it?

Right now, you're at a crossroads. At this crossroads, you're faced with two paths. Path one: you close the book, put it back on your shelf, and never think about it again. Path two: you commit to adopting a culture of love in your organization, and you share this book with everyone you can think of. Path one is easier, but it's also a dead end. Path two will set you and your organization on a journey of profound personal and professional transformation, but it will require sacrifice and hard work.

So, which path will you choose?

Obviously, you know which path we hope you will choose. But before you set out, let's take a moment to silence that voice in your head—the voice that says change is too hard, that says love will never work in your organization, that says you're only going to fail anyway.

The following are the most common excuses we hear from the many organizations, leaders, and team members who are hesitant to embrace a culture of love and bring humanity back to their workplace. If we're honest, they're also the same excuses we said and heard when we started out on this journey for ourselves.

We never said love was going to be easy. In fact, throughout each section of the book, we said the exact opposite. But here's the thing: nearly everything worth doing both in life and in business is hard. Only by embracing the challenge and confronting these excuses can we learn to move past them.

So buckle up. It's time for some tough love.

EXCUSE #1: OTHER CULTURE INITIATIVES DIDN'T WORK

"We've tried similar training before."

"Culture initiatives always fail."

"It's not going to stick."

We get these kinds of *been there, done that* responses a lot. At their core, these types of responses are rooted in unforgiveness for past initiatives that were dead on arrival. Maybe a trainer came to the office and ran a workshop; maybe the executive leadership team attended a weekend seminar; or maybe a consultant came and made a sincere effort to reshape the organization.

Whatever the specifics, the results are the same: a failed initiative.

No one likes it when things don't work out. But that doesn't mean you should stop trying. That doesn't mean change *can't* occur.

In our experience, it's our failed initiatives that have taught us the most—just look at our attempts to go Agile in the last chapter! We could have held onto that first bad experience and nixed any future calls to move forward. Instead, we took our lumps, learned our lessons, and made a better effort next time.

There are plenty of reasons why culture-based initiatives might fail. It could be that senior leadership was never bought in. It could be that the organization didn't choose the right consultants or program to lead the initiative. It could be that the initiative fizzled out because the change wasn't driven internally. Instead of harping on the bad, instead of dwelling on failure, learn from it and move forward.

Besides, most culture initiatives focus on surface-level aspects. They'll dust off their value statements, or they'll design new policies around diversity and inclusion. We applaud the intentions of these efforts, but most fail to get at the root problem: behaviors. If you haven't focused on behavior change, then you haven't truly had a culture initiative in the way we conceive of it. And here's the good news: when you focus on behaviors, the initiative is no longer about success or failure, but about progress.

EXCUSE #2: WE CAN'T AFFORD IT

Let's call this excuse what it is—a smokescreen. When someone says, "I can't afford it," they're really saying, "That's not important to me." They're scared. They're inflexible. They're consumed by that old-school corporate mentality of profit over people. Leaders like this will burn through money chasing new revenue opportunities. And yet the second someone utters the word "culture," suddenly they're tightening their purse strings and quoting revenue forecasts.

Let's be clear on two things.

First, the most important thing in your business is your people. Period.

Second, if you truly want something, you'll find the budget to pay for it. We're all rational to a degree, but often our money decisions come down to what we need or want at the moment.

We know from experience that culture transformations can be both expensive and time-consuming. Yes, it takes money to hire consultants. Yes, it takes money to attend seminars. Yes, it costs money to properly train and onboard your employees, to feed them and make them feel included, and to pay the additional cost for business-class tickets. But think of these expenses not as costs, but as *investments.* Executed with love and intention, these investments can pay off tenfold.

Don't believe us? Here's what we want you to do. First, ask yourself about all the costs you're ignoring—the cost of a high attrition rate, the cost of having little to no repeat business, and the cost of unaligned, ineffective teams. If you can, put a number to those costs—even if it's just a ballpark estimate.

Next, ask yourself how much more you can profit from a high-performing team, how many more revenue opportunities you'll earn through repeat business and word of mouth, and how much time you save when your leaders and your team members are aligned. Again, if you can, put a number to the value of those business outcomes.

Now look at the two numbers side-by-side. Still think it's not worth the investment?

In our experience, behaviors are the bottom line. The ROI of culture manifests in improved behaviors—and behaviors are what shift the numbers on the balance sheet. When you choose people over profit, your people choose you. The reward in business outcomes will more than make the investment worth it.

EXCUSE #3: CHANGE IS TOO HARD

The average person spends over 90,000 hours at work. Those in leadership positions often spend much more than that.

Yes, change is hard. But do you know what's harder?

Spending 90,000 hours in misery because you didn't speak up.

There's a big difference between hard and impossible. In our experience, the biggest difference between success and failure has nothing to do with the size of the challenge and everything to do with commitment. The more you are willing to commit, the more likely you are to succeed. It really is that simple.

Commitment is the hardest step on the path to change because it's the first. From there, each step gets a little easier. And the farther down the path you go, the more you realize you're not alone. After all, if commitment is anything, it's contagious. Once others see what you're trying to create, many will fall into step right alongside you.

EXCUSE #4: CHANGE TAKES TOO LONG

Today's business landscape is much different than it was in 2000, 2010, or even—dare we mention it—2020. Things happen faster. Every decision must be made yesterday. Course corrections must come swiftly and confidently.

That's what we're made to believe anyway. It's easy to get caught up in the instant gratification game, but the truth is, change still takes time. Ironically, that's the most consistent thing about change. If you pull the plug on an important initiative before it has a chance to work its magic, you do so at your own peril.

In other words, be patient.

Creating a culture of love doesn't happen in a day, a week, or even a year. It happens in small steps, in daily repetitions, in every moment of introspection where you commit to doing right by the people around you. It happens in small pockets, in seemingly unimportant moments, in everyday acts of putting the Six Pillars of Love to work.

Changing the behavior of one person is challenging and messy. Changing the behavior of an entire organization is even messier. Along the way, boundaries will get pushed. Relationships will be tested. Surprises will happen. But if you want lasting change, you must be willing to let these processes unfold at their own pace. If you try to rush things along—or worse, if you give up before you begin to see the results—you risk doing irreparable harm to your organizational culture. If you do, folks won't trust you—they won't care. And they'll be harder to convince the next time you try to roll something out.

EXCUSE #5: I'M NOT IN A LEADERSHIP ROLE

Once upon a time, there was a janitor named Richard Montañez who worked for the Frito-Lay snack company. One day in the late 1980s, he called the CEO and said that he had a great new idea for a product—Flamin' Hot Cheetos—that could help the company expand into the Latinx market. The CEO listened. Just a few years later, Montañez was the chief marketing officer for the entire organization, and one of the most respected executives in the snack industry.[10]

Everyone has a chance to make a difference in their organization. To think otherwise is to operate from a fixed mindset. Besides, you may not be a leader *yet*, but isn't that your plan— don't you want to get there eventually? Why not create some momentum around that plan by promoting a culture of love? What's the worst that could happen?

Here's some real tough love: If you're not willing to stand up for a better culture in your workplace, then you might as well stop complaining and get back to work. And if you *are* willing to stand up for a better culture and you get fired for it, then you probably shouldn't be working there in the first place. (Please let us know if you do get fired. If so, [1] sorry not sorry, and [2] we'd love to meet you.)

With that said, here's a word of encouragement. If you're a middle manager, you're actually in the perfect position to drive change from within.

To understand why, let us tell you about a concept we lovingly call the *crap umbrella*. Middle managers take a lot of crap. In a fear-based organization, that crap is raining down on them day in and day out. It's not a pretty sight, but it's also not inevitable.

When you embrace a culture of love, you get all the fringe benefits that come with it—including your very own crap umbrella. All you have to do is hold it over your head, open

---

10   Zachary Crockett. "How a Janitor at Frito-Lay Invented Flamin' Hot Cheetos." *The Hustle.*
     November 29, 2017. https://thehustle.co/hot-cheetos-inventor/

it up, and *voila*—you and your team are now protected from all the daily crap that has been raining down upon you.

That's a big deal. After all, it's easy to think that you don't have any influence as a middle manager. But to your team, you *are* the leader. Sure, they know that there are bosses above you, but you call the shots as far as their lives are concerned. Armed with your trusty crap umbrella, you can build an ecosystem of empathy, trust, and vulnerability for your team—so they don't have to deal with any of the s*** you're dealing with. And once your team knows that you're there to protect them, they'll be willing to move mountains for you.

Here's the other thing about the crap umbrella: it's always in style. As soon as someone else sees that you have one, they're going to want one too. Over time, crap umbrellas will start popping up all over the organization—until one day, just maybe, that rain of crap might cease altogether.

EXCUSE #6: THINGS AREN'T THAT BAD

This is the most dangerous excuse of them all—the biggest, most diabolical lie that leaders tell themselves. But ask yourself this: if things *really* aren't that bad, then why did you read this book all the way to the end?

Here's the truth. In a fear-based organization, when things go bad, leaders are usually the last to know. Tucked away in their executive suite, they're detached from every major issue, from every gripe, from every process. All the bad news is literally rebranded to look like good news—what folks call "the watermelon approach" (green on the outside, red on the inside). They mandate new rules and demand that their teams adopt new tools, but they don't have to follow or use any of them themselves—which means they have no idea what the lived experiences of their teams actually look like.

When you say, "Things aren't that bad," all you're really saying is that you're out of touch. And the moment your team members realize this, they will start formulating an exit strategy.

Besides, even if you know things are just going okay—not too bad, but not too great either—how long do you think "okay" is going to last? How long can you remain stagnant without losing ground in your market? How long before you are staring down your own darkest day?

Maybe for a little while. But not forever.

We get it: sometimes it feels safer to live with the problems you know than the problems you don't. It's a comforting thought, but it's also an illusion. In reality, staying put is often a much bigger risk than taking action. We stayed put for years—waiting until the last possible moment to change our culture—and we are fortunate to still be in business today. You don't have to be like us. You have an opportunity to change course now before the problems grow any worse.

THE TIME IS NOW

What you're feeling right now is the residual effect of tough love. It might not feel like it now, but that sting is good. After all, we'd be remiss if we got this far without telling it like it is. A critical conversation was in order, and if you remember way back in Chapter 1 and Chapter 2, we said that if you want to create a culture of love, then you've got to lean into the hard talks head-on so you can build a path forward together.

For too long, the corporate world has been stuck in old, outdated mindsets and unwilling to change. Today, whether we like it or not, that change is upon us. If the chaos and uncertainty brought by the COVID-19 pandemic have taught us anything, it's that business as usual isn't good enough anymore. In the face of great crisis, the organizations that exhibit the telltale signs of a culture of love—resilience, accountability, innovation—are best positioned to not only adapt and survive, but thrive.

When we struggle together, we learn together. When we learn together, we succeed together. Embracing our basic humanity and approaching our work with inclusion, trust, and empathy isn't a sign of weakness. It's a sign of strength.

But remember, change starts with you. If this is the future you want, then you have to create it. The good news is that you don't have to be the CEO or part of the executive leadership team to do it. No matter your role, no matter the current culture of your team, you have the ability to transform it.

It's a big task, but like any big task, it can be achieved in small steps. Here are the two most important steps to get started.

STEP #1: KNOW YOUR "WHY"

It's easy to think of change as a *what*. But look deeper. Remember your case for change (see Chapter 15). In our experience, lasting change always begins with *why*.

Everyone's *why* is different—and getting at your *why* requires self-awareness and introspection. Here are a few questions you can ask yourself:

Why do you need change? Why should you adopt new policies or practice the principles of leadership?

Who is this change for? A specific team or your entire organization?

If you could create an environment that was inclusive, supportive, and sustainable, what would that look like?

Why is this change worth it to you? To your company? Your employees and their families?

How do you want to be remembered? How can you change to help bring this about?

What would drive your team members to wake up every day and be excited to be a part of your team? What do they need to know to trust the change you're attempting to create? How can they be confident that the effort will pay off in the end?

Knowing your *why* is Step One. It's the crucial piece that every other aspect of a culture of love is built upon. Even more, it's your motivator to keep pushing forward when your efforts feel as if they have stalled—the superpower that will help you see past the small roadblocks and continue full-speed ahead.

You might know your *why* already. If you don't, focus on pointing yourself in the right direction. Ask yourself what change you want to see in your organization and why that's important to you. Start conversations with other leaders or team members. Share what you're thinking and invite their feedback. If you keep doing your work, your *why* will come to you—and if it changes as you move ahead, that's okay too.

STEP #2: MAKE MICRO-COMMITMENTS

Once you know your *why*, the next step is to start moving. Just remember, change never comes all at once. It might feel good to set out with a big, all-encompassing, life-changing goal—and we'd love to see you reach that goal.

But to get there, here's our advice: start small, make micro-commitments, and follow through. Over time, these small, incremental improvements will lead to big change.

When we say *micro-commitments*, we mean it. Itty-bitty baby steps. Create a goal so tiny, so seemingly insignificant that you'll have no excuse not to check it off your list. And be specific—even small goals usually involve a set of clear, actionable items.

Micro-commitments bring you small, tangible wins inside of a massive, abstract effort. It's much easier to commit to writing a single thank-you note to your colleague than it is to "build better relationships." The former commitment is specific and contained. The latter is so vague you won't know where to start, and often don't start because it feels too big to begin.

Further, it's easier to track your progress. You'll know full well whether you wrote a thank-you note on any given day—especially if you have an accountability partner to help keep you honest. By putting yourself in a position to succeed, you *will* succeed—and therefore, you'll be much, much more likely to keep the effort going.

To give an example, imagine that goal is to appreciate your team members more. That's a little abstract. Where do you even start? Turn it into a micro-commitment: "I will write a hand-written note to a different team member each day this week to thank them for their work." Even a commitment as small as that involves several steps to execution. First, you have to block out the time on your calendar (literally five minutes or less; there's no need to write them a novel). Then, you need to procure the necessary stationery (please don't overthink it). Finally, you have to reflect on your current projects and consider which team members might be going unnoticed (sometimes the hardest workers can fly under the radar).

The smaller you break a micro-commitment down to its component parts, the more likely you are to follow through—and therefore grow the culture of love within your organization. Then, once you've created a micro-commitment and made it a habit or checked it off your list, do another. And then do another after that. And another after that. And so on.

Through micro-commitments, we were able to turn the big ideas of love as a business strategy into small, daily wins. A culture of love is a mammoth idea—as are the Six Pillars we use to build it, and all the daily practices we've implemented throughout our organization. It has taken us years to turn this big idea into everyday reality. But the more micro-commitments we made, the more we celebrated the daily wins, the more our efforts snowballed into something bigger.

That's how a culture of love is built. Not in a day, but through everyday effort.

A NEW REALITY IS POSSIBLE

Whenever people ask us what Softway's focus is, we say it's to bring humanity back to the workplace. When many hear this, their first response is disbelief. What does that even mean? How is that even possible? Why would we even try to do that? The point of business is to make money—why would we care about humanity?

Here's our why: because business is personal.

For too long, we've brushed off the toxic cultures endemic in so many organizations. When someone is belittled, dehumanized, or fired, we brush it off as business as usual. As long as we embrace this mindset, as long as we tell ourselves this lie, then we are bound to it. That is our reality.

But it doesn't have to be. There is an alternative reality.

A reality where you can bring your full self to work, where you look forward to going to work, where you don't get Sunday anxiety (some folks call that feeling the "Sunday Scaries").

A reality where having a good time and being productive isn't mutually exclusive, where you know you can count on your team members for support, a reality where team members strive to do their best work—not out of fear of consequences, but for the fulfillment they get by being part of an engaged, inclusive team.

A reality where your well-being is truly in the interest of the company you work for, where you have a purpose and feel valued and respected, where you can grow, learn, and thrive.

A reality where you are valued for your difference in opinion, where you can truly be one person and not a work version and a home version, where you are included regardless of ethnicity, education level, religion, gender, country of origin, or political affiliation.

That is the reality we aspire to. That is the reality we work every day to create at our organization. That is the reality for the many other organizations that have traded in a culture of fear for a culture of love.

That can be your reality too. A reality where love is your business strategy.

If you're ready, we invite you to join us.

GETTING STARTED

As the old saying goes, "The best time to plant a tree was twenty years ago. The second-best time is now."

It's time to plant your tree and take a stand for love.

To help you on your journey, we've created a handy worksheet that will teach you everything you need to know about micro-commitments.

For this, and many more resources to help you adopt love as a business strategy, visit LoveAsABusinessStrategy.com.

ACKNOWLEDGMENTS

First and foremost, we would like to thank Softway employees past and present. To every person that has been a part of our company, every client, partner, and friend—thank you for being part of Softway's journey and for your dedication and support. To the folks that made this book possible, thank you. Chas Hoppe and Maggie McClurkin in particular, this book would not have been possible without your support and expertise.

FROM CHRIS PITRE

There is no such thing as a self-made man. Along with the many men who have supported and helped (including my father, Arthur D. Pitre, and my co-authors), I am especially grateful for the women who have poured into me. To the five women who have shaped my professional and personal conscience:

ALICE PITRE

My mom. The one who instilled in me the importance of detail orientation and efficiency in chores, education, and life.

PHYLLIS WIGGINS

My Pastor. The one who blessed me with wisdom, faith, and my first dose of introspection.

KANDACE COOKS

My sister. The one who taught me how to write, laugh, and lead. (This is the only place I'll admit that you taught me how to write.)

DR. LYNDA MADDOX

My favorite professor. The one who taught me the importance of self-editing, strategy, and the power of storytelling.

REBECCA ROGERS TIJERINO

My first executive mentor. The one who trained me in the art of selling, understanding financials, and ensuring alignment.

FROM JEFF MA

Every learning in this book is connected to some part of my personal journey. I've had difficult conversations, painful introspections, and some seriously bad behavior while trying to transform myself over the last few years. And through it all, no matter what, my amazing wife was always there holding my hand (both figuratively and literally). I could never have gotten here without her patience and encouragement. Even when I was at my worst, she never turned her back and always lifted me up. Thank you, Maggie, for your grace, your care, and your love.

In addition, I want to thank my co-authors. You guys are

basically brothers-in-arms to me. We have been through the trenches and seen it all together. Thank you for your constant love and support. A special thank you to Mohammad, who always saw the good in me—even when no one else did.

FROM MOHAMMAD ANWAR

Writing this book has been a blast, and I've had so much fun working with my co-authors and partners in crime—Chris Pitre, Frank Danna, and Jeff Ma. Thank you for agreeing to write this book with me and being a part of our journey here at Softway! I also want to thank Maggie McClurkin, without whom this book would not have been possible. Thank you for keeping us on track, holding us accountable, and making sure we had everything we needed to successfully write a book about a subject that we are so passionate about.

SHAKILA BEGUM AND ABDUL ANWAR (MOM AND DAD)

To my parents, I am extremely grateful and forever indebted to you both for all of your sacrifices and hard work that you've put in for our entire family and me. I am so grateful for the values you instilled in me and the effort it took to set a great example for how to live and lead my life. Love you, Mom and Dad!

KHALEEL ANWAR (BIG BRO), FAIZUN ANWAR (SIS), TAJ ANWAR (BRO), SIRAJ ANWAR (BRO)

I want to thank all four of my elder siblings for being my role models and protectors, and for being there for me no matter what I wanted to do. Your trust in me to lead Softway has allowed me to learn so much, and I will always be grateful to all of you for forgiving me for all the mistakes and blunders I have made along the way. Thank you, love you all!

YULIA PAKHALINA (SPOUSE)

Thank you to my beautiful wife! Many people may not see the sacrifices and the effort you put in to make sure that I am able to pursue my dreams with Softway, but I want you to know that I am eternally grateful for you and everything you do for our children and me. Without your support and cooperation—there wouldn't be a Softway. This journey thus far wouldn't have even been possible. Behind every successful man is a great woman. That great woman is you, Yulia, without you I wouldn't be able to achieve any of the success or continue to do so in the future. Thank you, love you!

SUFIA ANWAR AND MOHSIN ANWAR (CHILDREN)

Sufia and Mohsin—you have made me a better father, person, and human. Raising both of you has been an incredible joy and I look forward to what the future holds for both of you. Thank you for your unconditional love and support in everything that I set out to do. Love you both loads!

WAQAR FAIZ (MENTOR)

Thank you to my spiritual mentor, Waqar Faiz, for teaching me plenty of life lessons and for giving me a chance to introspect on my behaviors. Thank you for always being there to listen to me, hear me out, and give me the confidence and belief in anything that I needed to do. I am forever grateful for all of your teachings and encouragement.

SOFTWAY—PAST EMPLOYEES

To all the employees who have ever worked at Softway—thank you for your services and dedication. Thank you for giving me an opportunity to lead you all, but most importantly—I want to apologize to each and every one of you if I have hurt you or mistreated you (knowingly or unknowingly). I am grateful to each and every person that has been a part of Softway. You helped shape my perspective on my leadership and who I am as a person. Thank you!

SOFTWAY—CURRENT EMPLOYEES

To all the current employees who are by my side as we go forward on this journey to try and bring back humanity to the workplace—Thank You! Thank You for having faith and belief in our vision and purpose at Softway. Without you, I wouldn't even be a leader in the first place. I wouldn't be able to keep on this journey without all of your support, but also without you holding me accountable and for always being real with me and letting me hear what I really needed to hear. I am forever grateful to you all for your commitment, sacrifices, and hard work in this journey of ours! Thank you and love you all!

CUSTOMERS—PAST AND PRESENT

Thank you to all of my past and present clients! Thank you for entrusting Softway and me with solving problems and creating solutions for your organizations and teams. We value the opportunity you have given us and continue to give us to serve you and your team. I personally have learned a lot from each and every one of you. You all have been mentors to me in more ways than you know.

COACH TOM HERMAN

Coach, I have never spoken with you or met you! I don't know if I'll ever have a chance to meet with you, but you have been my mentor from the moment I saw you speak at a press conference on Nov 17th, 2015, when you spoke about your win as a Head Coach of the University of Houston Football victory over the University of Memphis Tigers that past Saturday. You taught me about a Culture of Love and what it means to be resilient and love your teammates. You gave me faith, hope, and belief for my own company and over 160 employees at that time when we didn't even know if we would survive and succeed and avoid having our company shut down or go bankrupt. I don't know if we would have survived as a business and thrived if it wasn't for your speech that day. I have watched you and modeled my own style of leadership and was inspired to create a Culture of Love inside our business because of you. You have helped me and our business in ways that you cannot imagine. But if you ever do read this book, I hope that you can see how much of an impact you have made on complete strangers—even off the field. I will forever be grateful to you and will always be your fan for life—because you changed my life and so many others! Thank You, Coach!

FROM FRANK E. DANNA

It's always been a dream of mine to write a book, a dream that started with me watching in awe as my late father, Charles Danna, furiously scribbled away at his manuscripts. He died before he was able to publish his novel, so Dad—thank you for inspiring me. There is no box.

TO MY WIFE

Megan, you are the most incredible person I've ever met. Your kindness, honesty, love, bravery, and brilliance are legendary. Over our incredible journey thus far, you've made me a better person and a better father. I married so far out of my league, y'all.

TO MY CHILDREN

Emma and Levi, I love you so much. You both make life worth living. Life is more colorful, joyful, and fun with you in it. I can't wait to see how each of you changes the world.

TO MOHAMMAD

You saw something in me that others didn't. You supported me from the sidelines, gave me chances when no one else would, and showed me what real inclusion looks and feels like. You taught me to pay opportunity forward. I won't let you down. Thank you for your friendship, and thank you for Softway.

TO MY CO-AUTHORS

Jeff, Chris, and Mohammad—you're not colleagues, you're family. The shade, the laughs, the heartbreak, and the triumph. We've been there for each other through thick and thin. Like the quality and craftsmanship of a pair of Adidas shoes, our bond will last a lifetime.

TO EVERYONE AT SOFTWAY PAST AND PRESENT

I love you all. Thank you for your dedication to this company and the work we're doing.

TO MY PARENTS (ALL OF YOU, MY AMAZING IN-LAWS INCLUDED)

Your support and encouragement are incredible. Thank you for believing in me.

TO MY FAMILY AND FRIENDS

The unconditional love that you share keeps me motivated.

TO DWAYNE "THE ROCK" JOHNSON

The world's busiest guy gets a shout-out here too. Your poise, integrity, and work ethic inspire me to be the hardest worker in every room.

FINALLY, TO YOU, THE READER OF THIS BOOK

You've taken time out of your life to learn a little more about our journey, and I hope you found real value in our stories and lessons. Thank you so much!

ABOUT THE AUTHORS

Mohammad, Chris, Frank, and Jeff are co-creators of the Seneca Leaders training experience and other culture-building products for Softway. Love as a Business Strategy is each author's debut book.

CHRISTOPHER JORDAN PITRE

Chris is a student of the world and enjoys anthropology, history, travel, and culinary experiences. His interests in global cultures naturally led him to travel around the world, co-facilitating Seneca Leaders, a leadership development training program, and managing client relationships globally. Chris is a native Houstonian who loves everything Beyoncé. He has a BA in Business Administration from The George Washington University in Washington, DC.

JEFFREY F. MA

Jeff spent the first decade of his career working in the video game industry, from game testing to project management. He continues to bring his love for games into everything he does, from playing with his kids to training and coaching leaders.

Jeff has a burning passion for board games, magic tricks, Agile, and growth mindsets. He was born and raised in Texas, where he and his beautiful wife, Maggie, dote heavily on their wonderful children, Cody and Penelope.

MOHAMMAD F. ANWAR

Mohammad is the youngest of five children and was born and raised in Saudi Arabia by Indian parents from Bengaluru. He graduated from the University of Houston (Go Coogs) with a BS in Computer Science and started Softway at twenty, where he still serves as the President and CEO.

Mohammad lives in Sugar Land, Texas, with his amazing wife Yulia, a Russian diver and five-time Olympic medalist, and his beautiful children, Sufia and Moshin. In his spare time, he enjoys fitness, watching college sports, and butchering American idioms.

FRANK E. DANNA

Frank, the oldest of six children, can often be found perfecting the art of brewing, drinking, and sharing coffee with friends and family. Frank is an entrepreneur at heart, having successfully sold his first startup at twenty-five.

Frank is a pop culture connoisseur, world traveler, and collector of limited-edition posters. In his spare time, he writes children's books, makes silly videos, and enjoys fitness. Frank lives in Houston, Texas, with his gorgeous wife Megan and awesome children, Emma and Levi.

ABOUT SOFTWAY

Softway is a business to employee (B2E) solutions company that offers experiences, services, and technology products to help build resilient, inclusive, and high-performing companies.

In 2015, when a toxic culture almost bankrupted the company, Softway's leadership team—including authors Mohammad Anwar (CEO), Chris Pitre (VP), and Frank Danna and Jeff Ma (Directors)—vowed to bring humanity back to the workplace. Through trial, error, and determination, they rebuilt their organization around their greatest asset: people.

Today, through the Seneca Leaders program and other employee-focused offerings, Softway is helping thousands of leaders spanning over forty-six countries transform their businesses by putting love to work.